BLOOD ON THE MOON

REEL WEST

REEL WEST

ANDREW PATRICK NELSON, SERIES EDITOR

Reel West is a unique series of short, neatly packaged volumes exploring individual Western films across the whole history of the canon, from early and classic Westerns to revisionist and spaghetti Westerns. The series considers the many themes and variations that have accrued over more than a century of this most American of film styles. Intended for general readers as well as for classroom use, these brief books will offer smart, incisive examinations of the aesthetic, cultural, experiential, and personal meaning and legacy of the films they discuss and will provide strong arguments for their importance—all filtered through the consciousness of writers of distinction from within the disciplines of film criticism, journalism, and literature.

Also available in the Reel West series:

Ride Lonesome by Kirk Ellis

Robert Mitchum as Jim Garry in *Blood on the Moon* (1948). His character could have traded in his Stetson and chaps for a fedora and raincoat (author's collection).

BLOOD ON THE MOON

ALAN K. RODE

University of New Mexico Press ∩ Albuquerque

Printed in the United States of America

Library of Congress Cataloging-in-Publication Data

Names: Rode, Alan K., 1954– author.
Title: Blood on the moon / Alan K. Rode.
Other titles: Reel West
Description: Albuquerque : University of New Mexico Press, 2023. |
Series: Reel West | Includes bibliographical references.
Identifiers: LCCN 2022037777 (print) | LCCN 2022037778 (ebook) |
ISBN 9780826364692 (paperback) | ISBN 9780826364708 (epub)
Subjects: LCSH: Blood on the moon (Motion picture) | Western films—
United States—History and criticism. | Film noir—United States—
History and criticism.
Classification: LCC PN1995.9.W4 R63 2023 (print) | LCC PN1995.9.W4 (ebook) |
DDC 791.43/75—dc23
LC record available at https://lccn.loc.gov/2022037777
LC ebook record available at https://lccn.loc.gov/2022037778

Founded in 1889, the University of New Mexico sits on the traditional homelands of the Pueblo of Sandia. The original peoples of New Mexico—Pueblo, Navajo, and Apache—since time immemorial have deep connections to the land and have made significant contributions to the broader community statewide. We honor the land itself and those who remain stewards of this land throughout the generations and also acknowledge our committed relationship to Indigenous peoples. We gratefully recognize our history.

Cover photograph: courtesy of the author's collection
Designed by Felicia Cedillos
Composed in Adobe Jenson 9.25/13.75

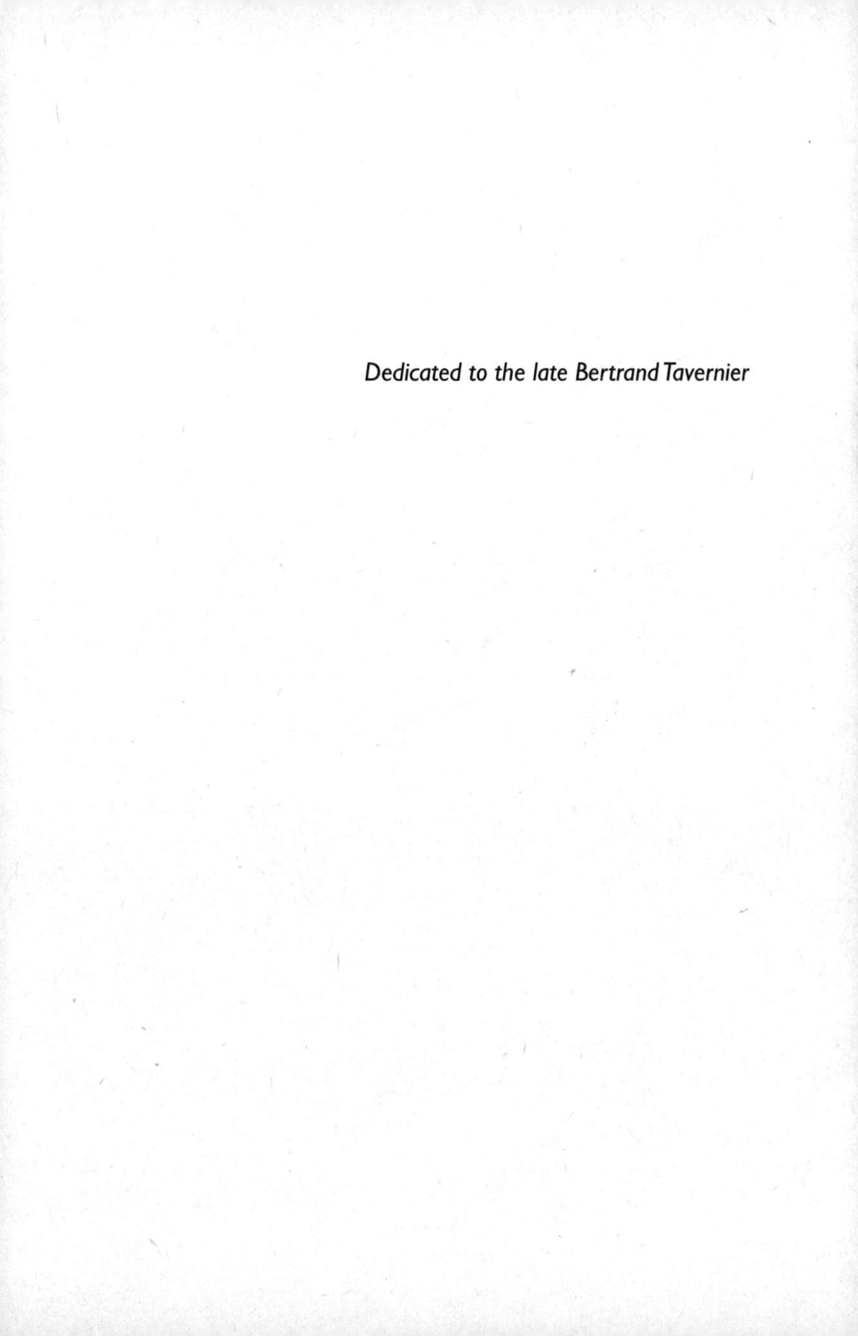

Dedicated to the late Bertrand Tavernier

CONTENTS

Italian *Blood on the Moon poster* (courtesy of the Brian Light Collection).

PREFACE

When classic Westerns are discussed or debated, *Blood on the Moon* is rarely, if ever, mentioned. Produced and released in 1948, the film received solid notices and was largely forgotten for nearly five decades. In addition to being a most formidable screen adaptation of the work of one the most renowned writers of Western fiction, *Blood on the Moon* was the forerunner of a hybrid genre, a cinematic orchid created via the propagation of the American Western with film noir.

Of movies categorized today as "noir Westerns," *Blood on the Moon* is at or near the top of the list. Produced during the height of the post–World War II film noir movement by RKO Pictures—a studio posthumously tabbed as "the capital of noir"—the film transplanted the dark urban environs of the city into the West's iconography. Instead of being heroically framed in a glorious Technicolor Monument Valley sunset, Robert Mitchum's lone horseman opens a resolutely black-and-white picture as a solitary figure in a dark rainstorm as an Arizona horse trail stands in for the rain-slicked streets of mid-twentieth-century Los Angeles. His existentialist character is at odds with the traditional Western hero's. He possesses nothing but a Stetson, a six-shooter, and a scant cattleman's outfit, a dilemma analogous to Philip Marlowe's self-inventory in *Farewell, My Lovely*: "a hat, a coat, and a gun." Akin to a Chandleresque private detective or a returning World War II veteran trudging through the back alleys and gilded neighborhoods of the apocryphal urban noir environment, Mitchum travels through a similarly alienating domain, where loyalties shift and things are assuredly not what they initially seem. Despite his Stetson and chaps, Mitchum's Jim Garry is the classic noir protagonist.

In the early stages of what would be a legendary career, director Robert Wise staged and filmed the picture in the classic noir style. The chiaroscuro lighting deployed during the claustrophobic interior scenes and at nighttime (constituting nearly half the running time) depicts isolated faces bathed in streams of light against a black background. Beyond its visual cast, the film is saturated with the narrative tropes of film noir. Behind the camera, the backstory of *Blood on the Moon* is as intriguing as the film itself. The screenplay was rescued from a stack of discards, and the picture subsequently boosted the careers of Wise and the iconic star Mitchum. Of keen historical interest, the film can be both understood and appreciated through the lens of retrospective assessment.

INTRODUCTION

Blood on the Moon was adapted from Luke Short's (real name Frederick Dilley Glidden) hard-bitten vision of the American West. Although Short's books were used for no fewer than eleven different Hollywood Western features, none was worthier than his serialized novel *Gunman's Chance*, which was retitled *Blood on the Moon*. The altering of the title connects the film to folklore surrounding the autumn "hunter's moon," which appears red, or to a total lunar eclipse, when wavelengths of red light bathe the lunar satellite in a reddish glow. Down through history, a "blood moon" has been considered a foreboding signal or a portent of doom—an apt description for the world in which Robert Mitchum's protagonist finds himself enmeshed. Glidden was different from most Western writers in that his literary style diverged toward noir themes. The late director and historian Bertrand Tavernier noted, "Luke Short, in fact, pulls the Western genre toward noir fiction, eschewing the usual Western hurdles and tropes, turning instead toward dark and confused sentiments, a heavy atmosphere full of repressed violence. . . . Many of his novels are built like investigations, far from any lyrical epic. The character slowly realizes what is really at stake and where he stands."[1] Brian Garfield, in his introduction to *Western Films: A Complete Guide*, dedicated the book to Glidden, putting the writer and his work in succinct

Author Fred Glidden found it much easier to accept a check from Aspen resident Earl Eaton than trying to earn a living as a nascent Hollywood screenwriter during the 1940s (courtesy of Aspen Historical Society; all rights reserved).

perspective: "He was a man to whom good and evil were absolutes but men and women were not."[2]

Blood on the Moon constitutes a cinematic melding of the Western, a film genre coinciding with the birth of cinema, and film noir, a stylistic movement emerging from Hollywood during and after World War II. Frederick Jackson Turner argued in his seminal 1893 thesis, "The Significance of the Frontier in American History," that the West shaped the

American characteristics of democratic opportunity and especially of individualism and violence during the nineteenth century. Though successive historians have argued that Turner's cultural hypothesis was specious and racially exclusionary, the influence of his theorem on the embryonic motion picture industry remains undeniable.

Beginning with Buffalo Bill's Wild West Show and dime novels, the West thrived as an idealized element of American popular culture. Edwin S. Porter's *The Great Train Robbery* (1903) established the Western as a foundational pillar of motion picture entertainment as the first "story film" with the narrative having a moral precept. Beginning with Broncho Billy Anderson and Cecil B. DeMille's *The Squaw Man* (1914), Western films captured the public's imagination as William S. Hart, Harry Carey Sr., and Tom Mix emerged as major stars. Although there were epics, including *The Covered Wagon* (1923) and *The Iron Horse* (1924), the advent of the Depression coincided with a hiatus of the Western blockbuster film. The early 1930s heralded the arrival of low-budget second features accompanied by the advent of the singing cowboy and Western serials. The genre would be restored to top-of-the-marquee status at the end of the decade with *Dodge City*, *Jesse James*, *Union Pacific*, and *Stagecoach*.

In a 1967 interview, director Anthony Mann described the Western as "legend—and legend makes the very best cinema. . . . It releases you from inhibitions, rules. . . . You can ride the plains, you can capture the windswept skies; you can release your audiences and take them out to places which they never dreamt of."[3] Mann's grandiose vision of the West as the ultimate backdrop for cinematic creativity is particularly intriguing when one recalls that he cut his directorial teeth while employed by the short-lived Eagle-Lion Films. Mann helmed several gritty urban noirs for Eagle-Lion: *T-Men* (1947), *Raw Deal* (1948), and *He Walked by Night* (partially;

1948), along with *Reign of Terror* (1949) (a.k.a. *The Black Book*) a movie about the French Revolution, which was produced in the noir style. These movies, strikingly photographed by Mann's visual doppelganger, director of cinematography John Alton, established both men's professional reputations. Mann and Alton would be hired away from Eagle-Lion in 1949 by Dore Schary, who, after leaving RKO when Howard Hughes bought the studio, ascended to become head of production at MGM. Mann and Alton were quite happy to leave the modestly budgeted Eagle-Lion features and the salaries that accompanied them in their respective rearview mirrors. What has been overlooked was how Mann, Alton, and other filmmakers established the American urban environment as a singular cinematic setting, whose style eventually merged with the Western—the most popular film genre for three-quarters of the twentieth century.

From the outset, Western films possessed unambiguous moral themes transposed against the wide-open spaces of the frontier, where life could be, in the words of Thomas Hobbes, "nasty, brutish, and short." Justice was often dispensed on an individualistic basis: a showdown between two rivals or a range war in which personal revenge and retribution became part of the natural order of things and the rule of law was abstract. It didn't matter whether the film dwelled on conflicts over control of the range, the construction of railroads, subjugating Native Americans by force, or gangs of outlaws running amuck; the delineation of characters as good or evil was crystal clear.

The Great Depression, followed by the New Deal, accelerated the country's transformation from an agrarian culture wedded to the memory of the frontier to a more modern social order that was denser, faster, and more urban. World War II proved to be an economic turbocharger for an increasingly transportive culture governed by laws and regulations rather than laissez-faire justice. The thematic reverie of the West, in which homesteaders resisted urban encroachment as represented by rustlers, unscrupulous ranchers, corrupt town leaders, or faro house grifters, was cinematically replicated with the advent of the gangster film. *Little Caesar* (1930) and *The Public Enemy* (1931) ushered in a genre that established a new urban frontier. The horse and the six-shooter were duplicated by the rum runner's truck and the tommy gun. "Ripped from the headlines" stories inspired by the real-life exploits of Al Capone, John Dillinger, the Barker Gang, et al. were rapidly produced into movies, most notably by Darryl F. Zanuck, Warner Bros.' head of production at the time. Many of the scripts and stories for the gangster films were penned by former big city reporters and urbanites, such as John Bright, Rowland Brown, Ben Hecht, and Jonathan Latimer, who had rubbed elbows with the actual mobsters. Prohibition, the federal government's spectacularly failed experiment in social engineering, fueled the rise of the urban gangster and racketeer as well as their concurrent portrayal on movie screens. Yet gangsters were clearly the bad guys, even if their spats and fedoras replaced the cowboy boots and black hats of their Western counterparts. The parish priest, the girl next door, and the incorruptible law enforcement figure fulfilled the roles of the honest sheriff, resolute homesteader, and rancher's daughter as the cinematic angels applying a figurative full nelson to the bad guys.

Beyond the commercial sensibility of filmmakers, some of whom stretched contemporary societal mores to the breaking point in selling movie tickets during the depths of the Depression, the distinction between good and evil on screen gained greater definition in the mid-1930s. After a series of Hollywood scandals and political pressure exerted by organizations including the Catholic Legion of Decency, the studios tethered themselves to the self-regulatory Production Code of 1930. The

Censor Joseph I. Breen was the undisputed puritanical pasha of American movie content for two decades. A zealous Catholic who was a true believer in the righteousness of the Production Code, Breen fought what ultimately became a losing battle in attempting to enforce outdated standards of morality and violence on screen (Urban Archives/Temple University and Thomas Doherty).

movie moguls viewed their acquiescence to the code as a last-ditch effort to avoid the likely possibility of their industry being regulated by the federal government. Enforcement of the Production Code wasn't vigorously pursued until July 15, 1934, when continued pressure from outside groups resulted in the appointment of Joseph I. Breen to head the Production Code Administration (PCA). The PCA replaced the good-old-boy network of movie moguls who sat on the Producers Appeal Board under the Motion Picture Producers and Distributors of America (MPPDA) umbrella and winked at each other regarding code enforcement. Breen was perfectly cast in the role of a reform sheriff with a coterie of obedient deputies, who roll up their sleeves to clean up a frontier Sodom and Gomorrah. His zealous enforcement of the Production Code consecrated him as the most powerful arbiter of commercial movie content for the following two decades.

Under Breen's administration, motion picture content become increasingly circumspect; topics including adultery, alcoholism, premarital sex, and other taboo subjects were severely constricted—if they could be portrayed on screen at all. Depictions of illicit drug use, violence deemed excessively brutal, and criminal acts such as counterfeiting and safecracking were forbidden. While sanitizing and approving every script submitted by the studios, Breen also denied reissue certificates to a host of so-called pre-code films that were released before his tenure began. Most critically, the already stark differentiation between good and evil on screen was now deemed inadequate to protect the public. A key extract from the Production Code summarizes the philosophy of how good and evil would be portrayed in movies: "That evil is not *presented alluringly*. Even if later in the film the evil is condemned and punished, it must not be allowed to appear so attractive that the audience's emotions are drawn to desire or approve so strongly that later the condemnation is forgotten and only the apparent joy of the sin remembered."[4]

Breen's January 19, 1938, missive to Jack L. Warner concerning James Cagney's portrayal of the gangster Rocky Sullivan in *Angels with Dirty Faces* (1938) was illustrative of this outlook. After pointing out that the *Angels* script included multiple violations of MPPDA policy concerning "Special Regulations on Crime in Motion Pictures," Breen added, "It is important to avoid any flavor of making a hero or sympathetic character of a man which at the same time is shown to be a criminal, a murderer and a kidnapper. In order to achieve this, great care will be needed both in the writing and actual shooting of the picture."[5]

In other words, evil movie characters could still be just that, but there were severe limitations on showing their bad acts, and they could never be portrayed with any mitigation or sympathy. No movie character could get away with murder, adultery, or many other lesser offenses. Glorification in crime pictures was usually reserved for members of law enforcement, particularly the Department of Justice and the nascent FBI under J. Edgar

Hoover, whose personal publicity machine elevated him to the exalted status of America's anticrime archangel. Thus many of the post–July 1934 gangster films, including *G-Men* (1935), *Dead End* (1937), *Each Dawn I Die* (1939), and *The Roaring Twenties* (1942), were essentially anticrime polemics. The conclusions of these pictures ensured wrong was always righted and was never glamorized, and those who committed bad acts either paid the price by dying or were otherwise punished. These boilerplate finales were part and parcel of what Breen defined as "compensating moral values,"[6] essential to maintaining proper standards of decency in American commercial filmmaking.

Even the fanatically determined Fritz Lang had to settle for an absurd cliché finale in *Fury* (1936), a startling noir forerunner involving mob violence and the supposed death of an innocent man, who returns to frame his would-be executioners. Subsequently hired by the independent producer Walter Wanger to direct *You Only Live Once* (1937), Lang tested the limitations of period directorial authority. Despite being given free rein to make the film, Lang had to fight his own screenwriters over inclusion of certain scenes of violence, and he personally supervised the re-editing of a bank robbery sequence to earn both the Breen office and the Ohio censor board's approvals. Despite the censorial interference, *You Only Live Once* provided a thematic template for future films noir such as *They Live by Night* (1949), *Gun Crazy* (1950), and *Bonnie and Clyde* (1967) by depicting a misunderstood or persecuted couple on the run from John Law and a vengeful society.

The intensive policing of movie content forced filmmakers to become more creative. A case in point was the seminal *Stagecoach* (1939). Director John Ford and screenwriter Dudley Nichols left no doubt that Claire Trevor's character was a prostitute, but there was next to nothing demonstrable in the script that the PCA could object to. John Wayne's climactic shoot-out with the man who killed his father and brother is presented as less an instance of vengeance and more an episode of frontier justice when Wayne, shouldering a rifle loaded with only three bullets, takes on a trio of murderous gunmen who confront him on the streets of Lordsburg. To be fair, Breen was more than a moralist attempting to convert the masses from his PCA pulpit. His missives served to protect the movie industry from the more punitive excesses of state and municipal censorship boards, whose perspectives often reflected a nostalgic yen for the revival of seventeenth-century Puritanism.

World War II ushered in a brief boom period for Hollywood. With more than 9 percent of the US population in uniform and millions more working in industries converted to defense, the war affected everyone in some form or fashion. The motion picture industry was federally regulated by the US Office of War Information (OWI) from June 1942 until September 1945. The OWI established the Bureau of Motion Pictures, which worked closely with the studios to champion and coordinate the production of war-themed propaganda films rolled out by Hollywood in assembly-line fashion. During the war years, everyone who could watched the movies. But by 1943, the grim reality of the war initiated a transition in movie content, despite the Production Code. Beyond wartime propaganda films leavened by lighter fare, such as Abbott and Costello comedies and Preston Sturges's *The Miracle of Morgan's Creek* (1944), along with horror and fantasy pictures and war-themed inspirations like *Casablanca* (1942) and *So Proudly We Hail* (1943), movies began to address the darker dimensions of the human condition.

The Ox-Bow Incident (1943) was a groundbreaking Western that explored the ambiguities of the participants in a lynching. Though Lamar

Trotti's screenplay (adapted from Walter Van Tilburg Clark's novel) portrayed the set piece lynching as a singularly evil act, the motivations of the various participants were complex and ambivalent. Alfred Hitchcock's *Shadow of a Doubt* (1943) related the nightmarish tale of a beloved uncle visiting his traditional small-town California family. Unfortunately, good old Uncle Charlie turns out to be a serial murderer of rich widows. The following year brought forth what would later be viewed as a new and different style of Hollywood movie. Of those 1944 releases, *Double Indemnity*, adapted from James M. Cain's novel, was a case in point of how censorship battles between the movie studios and the Breen office could be lost and then won as the war began to loosen cultural mores.

Cain's novel as adapted for the screen stars an insurance salesman (Fred MacMurray) who has an affair with a southern California oil contractor's wife (Barbara Stanwyck) and then colludes with her to murder her husband to collect on an insurance policy; the plot immediately raised hackles at the PCA. In what would come to be a classic noir trope, the salesman is an otherwise honest man who succumbs to temptation to commit murder for a woman and the insurance money, even though he knows it is legally and morally wrong. After Cain's novel was published in serial form in 1935, MGM offered him $25,000 for the movie rights but reneged because of pressure from Breen, who emphatically believed Cain's story was morally unsuitable for any type of movie adaptation. Eight years later, after *Double Indemnity* was published as a novel, Cain accepted $15,000 from Paramount (Breen's machinations effectively cost Cain $10,000); Billy Wilder and Raymond Chandler fashioned a script that barely scraped under the PCA's censorship limbo bar. Cain was originally a newspaper writer who went to Hollywood to scribe for the movies, but he never acquired the knack for effective screenwriting. His novels were a different matter. The world according to Cain was a blunt instrument lashed together by untidy people, dark corners, and bad endings. His unique style of first-person narration, characterized by the absence of formal dialogue identification, constituted a new form of popular literature. His work was perfectly timed to be in the vanguard of the post–World War II film noir movement. But what exactly was film noir?

The Italian-born French movie critic Nino Frank is credited with using the term *film noir* to describe a group of American films screened in French movie theaters for the first time after the war in the summer of 1946: *The Maltese Falcon* (1941), *Laura* (1944), *Murder, My Sweet* (1944), *The Woman in the Window* (1944), and *Double Indemnity* (1944). Frank's article "Un nouveau genre 'policier': L'aventure criminelle" ("A New Police Genre: The Criminal Adventure") was published in the socialist-leaning film magazine *L'Écran Français* in August 1946. Frank's article listed "rejection of sentimental humanism, the social fantastic, and the dynamism of violent death" as being obsessive French noir themes and called attention to the American proclivity for "criminal psychology and misogyny." He further wrote, "These 'dark' films, these films noir, no longer have anything in common with the ordinary run of detective movies."[7] Lee Horsley wrote in *The Noir Thriller*, "Nino Frank's article reflects the difficulty of finding a suitable label for these 'dark films.'"[8]

Frank elaborated that the noir films "belong to what used to be called the detective film genre, but which would now be better termed the crime, or, even better yet, the 'crime psychology film.'" In a November 1946 essay titled "Les Américains aussi font des films 'noirs'" ("The Americans Also Make 'Black' Films") in the conservative-leaning *Revue du cinema*, Jean-Pierre Chartier criticized what he deemed the common thread of film noir: "pessimism and disgust for humanity." Frank's and Chartier's use of the term *film noir* may have been inspired by the *Série Noire*, Gallimard's series of "hard-boiled" detective and crime fiction.

Of course, at the time, no one in Hollywood knew what film noir was or what the term meant. Noir wasn't written about or discussed by American critics and filmmakers until the 1960s. Period filmmakers and the public tabbed these stylistic movies as "mysteries," "suspensers," "thrillers," "crime dramas," or the catchall "mellers," denoting melodramas. Film noir was a retrospective realization of a unique cinematic style with roots emanating from several different sources.

Hard-boiled detective fiction writers, including Dashiell Hammett, Raymond Chandler, and Cain, broadened their audiences. From 1920s-era pulp fiction magazines that serialized their work, they moved on to mainstream-published books, which became popular and were bought by movie studios for screen adaptations. Hammett was the first hard-boiled writer to be firmly established on the big screen, with three different screen versions of *The Maltese Falcon* (1931, 1936, and 1941), two versions of *The Glass Key* (1935 and 1942), and the hugely successful *Thin Man* films at MGM beginning in 1934. By contrast, in 1942 Chandler's novels *Farewell, My Lovely* and *The High Window* were initially shoehorned into RKO's low-budget Falcon mystery series (*The Falcon Takes Over*) and Fox's Michael Shayne (*Time to Kill*) programmers, which gave rise to the enduring myth that film noir consisted primarily of B movies.

Cornell Woolrich, a writer who lived a wretched existence seemingly lifted from one of his fearfully paranoid tales, began selling his short stories and novels to Hollywood in 1938. After hitting his stride with his novels being adapted for *Phantom Lady* (1944), *Deadline at Dawn* (1946), and *Black Angel* (1946), Woolrich (who also wrote under the pen names George Hopley and William Irish) ended up being the most prolific of all mystery writers whose work has been adapted for the screen. But hard-boiled writing isn't always noir. It is often an extension of the traditional Western motif wherein the protagonist is a detective or a cop whose ethics are governed not always by the rule of law but by a personal code of rectitude. In the end, the hero does the right thing and normalcy is reaffirmed after several plot twists, often accompanied by an equivalent number of corpses.

What became socially significant was how the noir style reflected the changing ethical and cultural mores of the country as postwar realism began to insinuate itself into Hollywood films. Writer Jon Tuska defined film noir as "a darkling vision of the world . . . a view from the underside, born of fundamental disillusionment perhaps, but also invariably the result, no matter how timid, of a confrontation with nihilism."[9] Existential nihilism is shorthand for life having no meaning, purpose, or value other than existence. Robert Porfirio wrote that noir essentially has "an underlying mood of pessimism which undercuts any attempted happy endings and prevents the films from being the typical Hollywood escapist fare many were originally intended to be. More than lighting or photography, it is this sensibility which makes the black film black for us."[10] At its core, noir's dark sensibility is minimalist. The opening of *The Killers* (1946) is a case in point. Burt Lancaster offers a terse explanation of why he, a down-and-out ex-boxer, now a nondescript filling station attendant, was about to be murdered by two professional hitmen: "I did something wrong . . . once."

World War II exposed the horrific realities of global carnage as engineered by Hitler, Mussolini, and the Japanese militarists, culminating with the mass destruction and cost in human lives necessary to defeat them. For those personally untouched by the devastation, there were theater newsreels of the battlefield dead. *With the Marines at Tarawa* (1944)—a film codirected by actor Louis Hayward and personally authorized by

President Roosevelt, who overrode Breen and an array of state and local censor boards so it could play in movie theaters—broke the ice by revealing grim realities of the war that were unrelated to any heroic sanitization of conflict depicted in Hollywood propaganda films. The horrific destructive power of US atomic bombs, followed by the postwar revelations of the Nuremburg trials and the establishment of the United Nations, introduced the word *genocide* into the popular lexicon. The twentieth century was unofficially recognized as the epoch of mass slaughter.

Crossfire (1947) and *Gentleman's Agreement* (1947) broke new ground by addressing the topic of anti-Semitism. These films would never have been considered commercially viable before the war. It would take until the end of the decade for Hollywood to produce any movies touching on racism, the third rail of America's segregated society, with *Home of the Brave* (1949), *Lost Boundaries* (1949), and *No Way Out* (1950). Historically, it can be argued, several war-themed films produced during the conflict's recent aftermath, such as *Twelve O'clock High* (1949) and *The Men* (1950), were much more realistic than the idealized Steven Spielberg nostalgia jams about "the good war" emerging on screen and television many years later. A decade after VJ Day, it was left to film noir to provide perhaps the starkest instance of wartime angst when Frank Sinatra was cast as a Silver Star–winning army combat hero who becomes a postwar killer for hire attempting to assassinate the US president in *Suddenly* (1955).

The average person might not have pondered the definition of "existential nihilism," but the war compelled people to grapple with the meaning of their own lives. With thousands of Americans in uniform returning to a changed country, where women either served or worked full-time and otherwise supported the home front, movies depicting married couples sleeping in separate beds or not being allowed to kiss with genuine passion harked back to a bygone era of whalebone corsets and buggy whips.

The Cold War emerged as Joseph Stalin made a veritable costume change, from "Uncle Joe" to the dictatorial "Man of Steel," constructing an Iron Curtain across Europe. The legitimate concern over the expansion of Soviet totalitarianism enabled right wing zealots in America to whip up an irrational maelstrom of fear and loathing about domestic communism. The war caused those who experienced it to question their existence—as well as the motivations and actions of others. Almost subconsciously, postwar movie audiences had an expectation of greater realpolitik concerning dramatic situations depicted in Hollywood films, even in idealized Westerns.

The Gunfighter (1946), with a screenplay originally written by William Bowers for John Wayne, instead starred Gregory Peck as Jimmy Ringo, an outlaw who discovers being a fast gun is akin to having a target on his back. Everyone wants to try him, and as the bodies mount up, Ringo has fewer options. He reunites with his estranged wife and a young son, who doesn't know him, in an attempt to establish a normal life. But his gunslinging celebrity confines him to sitting in a saloon with his back against the wall; the notoriety of his exploits ultimately costs Ringo his life. A film that would be widely imitated, *The Gunfighter* displaced the heroism myth often associated with Westerns while thematically capturing the postwar weariness that deglamorized occupational killing.

Joseph Breen was astute enough to realize he was now waging a losing battle in attempting to freeze-frame American morality. Celluloid whimsy, including the Andy Hardy series at MGM and the Maria Montez–Jon Hall sword-and-sandal epics at Universal, disappeared from movie screens. America had reached its majority, and the postwar movie industry had to play catch-up. From a sociological perspective, film noir was a cinematic movement for a generation that was compelled to come of age more rapidly than its predecessors.

The Gunfighter (1950). Much to his chagrin, Gregory Peck discovers that becoming a renowned fast gun constitutes entry into a postmortem popularity contest (author's collection).

While detective fiction and postwar cultural changes definitively left their imprint, film noir was an essentially visual style with European origins. Most of the movies originally classified as film noir were directed by men who participated in German or European cinema during its peak era of 1919 to 1933. These directors include Fritz Lang, Billy Wilder, Robert Siodmak, William Dieterle, Douglas Sirk, Otto Preminger, Jacques Tourneur, Max Ophüls, and Curtis Bernhardt. Michael Curtiz, a Hungarian émigré who came to America in 1926 after directing more than seventy films on the continent, is also a member of this ensemble. Many of these men fled Hitler and the Nazis during the 1930s. The theatrical tradition and respect for literacy in Germany and Western Europe shaped an emotional expressionism in post–World War I European films. *The Cabinet of Dr. Caligari* (1919) is considered the first German expressionist film, with its twisted stairways, distorted buildings, and shadowed lighting, accentuated by the period extravagance of the acting. This style—also attributable to the influence of the stage director Max Reinhardt and Weimar "street films"—bled into the films noir of the 1940s and their emphasis on chiaroscuro lighting portraying the city at night: shadows of buildings and people, distorted characters and images, oblique and vertical lines of light through staircases, venetian blinds symbolizing entrapment amid blinking neon signs, and faces backlit and shot at different angles to convey an ominous mood.

Film noir was inspired by German cinema and its participants, but French films during the 1930s also creatively shaped the noir style and sensibility. Jean Renoir's *La chienne* (1931), about a woman and a pimp exploiting a henpecked amateur painter, would be remade by Lang as *Scarlet Street* (1945), a seminal entry in the film noir canon. Marcel Carné's *Jenny* (1936), *Port of Shadows* (1938), and *Hotel du Nord* (1938) and Julien Duvivier's *Pépé le Moko* (1937) were the predecessors of the postwar fatalistic French noirs made by Duvivier (*Panique*), Henri-Georges Clouzot (*Quai des Orfèvres*, *The Wages of Fear*, *Diabolique*), and Yves Allégret (*Such a Pretty Little Beach*, *Manèges*). These and other films produced in Mexico, Argentina, and elsewhere illustrate how noir became an international cinematic movement. Although European directors imparted much of the noir style to Hollywood movies, it was quickly replicated and expanded on by American filmmakers who were already making studio films; Hollywood has always been a more imitative entity than a creative one. Over time, definite film noir conventions and tropes were established. While creating an all-inclusive list for a cinematic style ascertained by subjective criteria such as tone and motif (or, as suggested by Paul Schrader, a specific cycle rather than a genre) is akin to squaring a circle, these elements include:

- A twentieth-century urban setting, often at night, featuring rain or rain-slicked streets
- Interiors that are gloomy, shabby, and depressing

- Characters who are morally ambiguous, unhappy, dissatisfied, unattained, or lost
- Amnesia, "film noir's version of the common cold,"[11] often used as a characterization or plot point for a noir protagonist
- An absence of comedic humor unless it is cynical, wry, or corrosive in nature
- Defiance of the law and existing social mores by the protagonist or other characters
- Fatalism characterized by a transgression that evolves into an out-of-control situation
- Low-key, dark-shaded, and shadowed lighting and photography such as deep-focus or depth-of-field camera shots that accentuate elements of bleakness, mistrust, despair, entrapment, and paranoia
- Corrupt or indifferent law enforcement characters and antiheroic characters
- A femme fatale who is often contrasted by loyal, loving female characters
- Complicated narratives often related via voice-over narration and flashbacks

But it was the cinematographers who created the photography associated with noir. A non-inclusive list of these artists is headed by the aforementioned John Alton, along with Burnett Guffey, John Seitz, Theodor Sparkuhl, Nicholas Musuraca, Joseph LaShelle, Lee Garmes, Woody Bredell, Milton Krasner, and the legendary James Wong Howe, among others. It is not coincidental that two of the initial Westerns definitively produced in the noir style, *Pursued* and *Blood on the Moon*, were filmed by Howe and Musuraca.

Pursued (1947), a dark Freudian tale of Western family dysfunction, concludes with star Robert Mitchum (almost) at the end of his rope (author's collection).

Pursued, released in February 1947, opens with Jeb Rand (Robert Mitchum) shown in flashback as boy of four witnessing the brutal murder of his mother and father in the 1880s Southwest while hiding under the floorboards of their house. He is lovingly adopted by a nearby family (Judith Anderson, Teresa Wright, and John Rodney) but remains forever haunted by his memory. Jeb becomes romantically involved with his stepsister, Thor (Wright), but his competitive relationship with his stepbrother, Adam (Rodney), turns venomous when abetted by the machinations of a vengeful Uncle Grant (Dean Jagger), who spends virtually the entire movie attempting to murder Jeb. Jeb ends up killing his stepbrother in self-defense and then Thor's frustrated suitor (Harry Carey Jr.), who tries to assassinate him. Thor then marries Jeb in order to kill him in revenge on their wedding night, but she can't go through with it. It turns out that Uncle Grant is attempting to avenge his sister's affair with Jeb's father. Jeb is rescued at the eleventh hour when Ma (Anderson) kills Grant, who is preparing to hang Jeb from a nearby tree.

This story of murderous Freudian dysfunction was penned by screenwriter Niven Busch as a vehicle for Teresa Wright, who was his wife at the time. Although the picture is dark to its core, the script morphs into an overwritten saga of noir family values (the Uncle Grant character has no explanatory depth beyond being a sadistic ignoramus), as decades of familial bloodshed are a preferable alternative to Ma's simply telling Jeb about her affair with his father, which created her brother's decades-long mad vengeance. *Pursued* was directed on location in Gallup, New Mexico, with great flair by Raoul Walsh. James Wong Howe's photography was superb, although he often resorted to using day-for-night camera filters rather than filming at night.

Ramrod, released in May 1947 by United Artists, was the fledgling production of Enterprise Productions, Inc. Frederick Glidden's story (written under his Luke Short pen name) was initially serialized and subsequently published by Macmillan in 1943. The book was adapted by Jack Moffitt, C. Graham Baker, and Cecile Kramer, a trio of unremarkable screenwriters who wisely left much of the novel intact. Glidden's talent for characterization—so well suited for the big screen and the postwar noir movement—was deftly handled by director André De Toth, who understood the benefits of a fast narrative tempo to cogently relate a story on screen.

The cinematographer was Russell Harlan, a former stuntman and an accomplished photographer of Westerns, beginning with the 1930s Hopalong Cassidy films. The Cassidy oaters were produced by Harry "Pop" Sherman, who by no small coincidence was also the producer of *Ramrod*. Harlan, who became Howard Hawks's favorite cameraman after filming *Red River* (1948), was better known for his stunning iconography of expansive mountain vistas and western skylines than for the backlighted

Ramrod (1947) Joel McCrea appears to be in charge of Don DeFore, Ray Teal, Hal Taliaferro, and Wally Cassell, but the actual boss is Veronica Lake in a singular portrayal of calculating ruthlessness (author's collection).

urban environs of the city. Nonetheless, Harlan earned his noir credentials in 1950 with *Gun Crazy* and *Southside 1-1000*, with his subsequent work being nominated for the Best Cinematography Academy Award five times. *Ramrod* was filmed in Utah's Zion National Park, as De Toth believed locations were just as important as actors. His view was that the spectacular Zion location was beyond mere scenery and went to the heart of the film's narrative: "the harshness, the cliffs, the river. It was real."[12]

Even with that, it was the story that elevated *Ramrod* into the vanguard of noir-stained Westerns. Having cast Joel McCrea as the lead, Enterprise borrowed Veronica Lake from Paramount. The plot initially seemed to be a typical range war story until Lake's character, Connie Dickason, takes matters into her own hands. After her sheep drover fiancé, Walt (Ian MacDonald), is forced out of town by the formidable cattle rancher Frank Ivey (Preston Foster), Dickason hires David Nash (McCrea), defies her father (Charlie Ruggles) to bring in cattle, and arranges a stampede to incriminate Ivey. Instead, her mayhem causes the deaths of several innocent men. During her subsequent campaign of manipulating men in a freewheeling orchestration of assorted double-crosses to get what she wants, Connie's ruthlessness outstrips Lake's ostensible femme fatale portrayals in *This Gun for Hire* (1942), *The Glass Key* (1942), and *The Blue Dahlia* (1946). In the end, Nash realizes his employer's callous machinations have killed both the local sheriff (Donald Crisp) and his gunslinging pal (Don DeFore). He rejects her romantic blandishments for the encircling arms of the film's "good" woman (Arleen Whelan). Despite her murderous excesses, Connie Dickason is spared the Production Code's ritualistic "compensating moral values" death sentence and instead is left bereft of the man she wanted and looks gloomily to an uncertain future.

André De Toth, whose marriage to Veronica Lake foundered as her life tragically spiraled into alcoholism and drug addiction, became a director noted for his noir style. As one critic summarized, "Like fellow European émigrés Fritz Lang and Robert Siodmak, de Toth brought a grim, harsh, even brutal sensibility to the studio material he was given. He gravitated naturally to *film noir* (*Pitfall*, 1948, and *Crime Wave*, 1954, are probably his strongest), and that *noir* perspective also comes through in his numerous vividly staged Westerns."[13]

Fostered by the aforementioned historical events and societal changes, as systemized by a diverse number of movies and their makers, film noir's permeation of Western movies achieved a comprehensive realization in *Blood on the Moon* in 1948. The film is decisively in the vanguard of a different style of Western produced during the postwar period. *Blood on the Moon* also remains historically emblematic concerning the regression

Robert Bray grudgingly extends a helping hand to Robert Mitchum after an opening cattle stampede in *Blood on the Moon* (author's collection).

of the Hollywood studio system and the attitudinal changes in American popular culture.

What follows is a synopsis and accounting of how and why the film was made, including a detailed analysis of the author, a discussion of the evolution of the screenplay, and comprehensive overviews of the director, the studio, the cast, and the production and postproduction histories. *Blood on the Moon* was one of the last features green-lighted by RKO's production head Dore Schary before the eccentric tycoon Howard Hughes took control of the studio, only a month after the film wrapped in May 1948. The picture heralded the emergence of director Robert Wise, who would join Hollywood's pantheon of film directors amid the chaotic history of RKO Pictures—before, during, and after its demise under Hughes—while boosting the star ascent of the emerging Robert Mitchum.

A sodden Mitchum encounters the suspicious duo of Bud Osborne and Tom Tully (author's collection).

SYNOPSIS

Blood on the Moon opens with "down on his uppers" Jim Garry (Robert Mitchum) nearly trampled by a herd of runaway steers while camping on Indian reservation rangeland. Garry—a stranger—is questioned by the herd's owner, John Lufton (Tom Tully). The mistrustful Lufton reveals that after years of supplying the local Ute reservation with beef, he is being forced out by Jake Pindalest (Frank Faylen), the new Indian agent. Lufton is also fighting Tate Riling (Robert Preston), who has organized area farmers to prevent him from moving his cattle back to the basin grazing land that was once his but has been opened up to homesteaders. Although suspicious that Garry may be one of Riling's hired guns, Lufton asks him to deliver a note to his family. As Garry approaches the Lufton ranch, he is shot at by a woman, who turns out to be Lufton's daughter Amy (Barbara Bel Geddes). After Garry hands the note to Lufton's elder daughter, Carol (Phyllis Thaxter), he is summarily dismissed by Amy and Lufton's ranch foreman.

He rides into the local town of Sundust and is misidentified as a Lufton ally and nearly killed by Riling's farmers, led by the volatile Milo Sweet (Charles McGraw). While running away, Garry spots Carol Lufton throwing a rock with a note attached through a hotel window. Garry is saved by none other than Tate Riling, who is revealed to be an old friend who summoned Garry to Sundust help him fight Lufton. Riling reveals to Garry that his actual plan is not to liberate land for the farmers but to force Lufton, who must soon vacate the reservation, to sell his cattle to him at a cut-rate price and then sell the herd to Pindalest, with whom he is in cahoots, at an inflated cost. Because he is broke, Garry agrees to become Riling's lead henchman and partner, but he evinces little enthusiasm for the scheme.

The next day, Carol and Amy Lufton ride to meet their father at the basin crossing point. When they arrive, however, they are greeted by Riling, a pair of hired guns, Garry, and the homesteaders. Amy reveals that her father deliberately wrote the wrong location on the note and angrily accuses Garry of betraying its contents. Unknown to Amy, Carol, who is in love with Riling, was the source of the information and later agrees to tell her lover where her father actually crossed. Soon after, as Amy informs Lufton about Jim Garry being a Riling hired gun, Riling and his men storm into Lufton's cattle camp and start a stampede. During the ensuing chaos, one of Lufton's cowboys is trampled to death and a homesteader, Fred Barden, is shot. A saddened Garry informs Fred's father, Kris (Walter Brennan), a Riling supporter, about his son's death and then rides into Sundust. There Garry saves Lufton's life when he is almost gunned down in cold blood on the main street by Frank Reardon (Tom Tyler) and Joe Shotten (Clifton Young), Tate Riling's hired guns. After a grateful Amy apologizes to him, Garry leaves town.

While pausing at a commissary saloon, Garry is confronted by Riling, who now wants him to make the purchase offer to Lufton. Disgusted by his friend's avariciousness and manipulation of Carol Lufton, Garry calls him out. The two men fight each other savagely until Garry knocks Riling

Jim Garry's reception committee at Lufton's ranch isn't ready to roll out the welcome wagon. Left to right: Phyllis Thaxter, Barbara Bel Geddes, and Tom Keene (author's collection)

unconscious. The exhausted, wounded Garry is saved by Kris Barden, who shows up and shoots Reardon in the back just as the gunslinger prepares to murder Garry. Returning to the Lufton ranch, Garry reveals Riling's plot to Amy and her father as Amy tends to his injuries. Garry suggests he can delay Pindalest's deadline by a week, enough time for the rancher to round up his now-scattered cattle. Believing that Garry intends to murder the Indian agent, Lufton refuses his offer. Garry leaves the ranch in a huff. Amy follows Garry and convinces him to execute his plan with Pindalest. To that end, Garry confers with the agent at the reservation and, posing as

Riling's go-between, tells him that his partner is demanding $3,000 more for Lufton's cattle.

The suckered Pindalest declares that he must go to town for the extra cash. Once he and Garry are in the open range, the cowboy reveals that he has switched sides and intends to hold the agent captive until Lufton has rounded up his cattle. The next morning, however, as a snowstorm blows in, Garry is ambushed and knifed by an Indian who works for Riling. Garry eventually overwhelms the Indian, but Pindalest escapes. A badly wounded Garry flees to Kris Barden's ranch. Amy soon arrives there and insists on fighting Riling, Reardon, and Pindalest, who have surrounded the Barden ranch. As the gunfight ensues, Garry regains enough strength to sneak out of the ranch house to kill Reardon and knock Pindalest unconscious. Garry then outdraws Riling, who dies in his arms. With Pindalest in the custody of the sheriff, Garry and Amy toast their impending marriage with a delighted Lufton and the reunited ranchers and homesteaders.

CREDITS FOR *BLOOD ON THE MOON*

RELEASE DATE

Released November 9, 1948 (New York City premiere)

COPYRIGHT DATE

November 10, 1948

RUN TIME / ASPECT RATIO

88 minutes / 1:37:1

DISTRIBUTED BY

RKO Radio Pictures Inc.

PRODUCTION COMPANY

RKO Radio Pictures Inc.

EXECUTIVE PRODUCER

Sid Rogell

PRODUCER

Theron Warth

DIRECTOR

Robert Wise

SCREENPLAY

Lillie Hayward

Harold Shumate (adaptation)

Frederick D. Glidden (adaption; under the pen name of Luke Short)

Based on the novel *Gunman's Chance* by Luke Short (New York, 1941)

PHOTOGRAPHY

Nicholas Musuraca (director of photography)

Fred Bentley (camera operator)

Ollie Sigurdson (stills)

ART DIRECTOR

Albert D'Agostino

Walter E. Keller

COSTUME DESIGN

Edward Stevenson (gowns)

Robert Richard

TECHNICAL ADVISOR
Joe De Yong

EDITOR
Samuel E. Beetley

SET DECORATORS
Darrell Silvera
James Altwies

SOUND
John L. Cass
Terry Kellum

MUSIC SCORE
Roy Webb (composer)
Gilbert Grau (orchestration)
C. Bakaleinikoff (musical director)

VISUAL EFFECTS
Russell A. Cully

MAKEUP
Gordon Pau (makeup supervisor)
Webster Phillips (makeup—Sedona location)
Hazel Rogers (hair stylist)

PRODUCTION MANAGEMENT
Edward Killy (production manager)
Bill Shanks (script supervisor)
Tom Clement (grip)
Maxwell O. Henry (assistant director)
Joel Freeman (assistant director)
Arthur Rosson (second unit director)
Theron Warth (second unit director)
Edward Kelly (second unit camera)
Jack MacKenzie (second unit camera)
Clifford Stine (assistant)

STUNTS/RIDERS
Gil Perkins
Ted Mapes
Carl Saxe
James Van Horn
Ruth Brennan

CAST

Robert Mitchum	*Jim Garry*
Barbara Bel Geddes	*Amy Lufton*
Robert Preston	*Tate Riling*
Walter Brennan	*Kris Barden*
Phyllis Thaxter	*Carol Lufton*
Frank Faylen	*Jake Pindalest*
Tom Tully	*John Lufton*
Charles McGraw	*Milo Sweet*
Clifton Young	*Joe Shotten*
Tom Tyler	*Frank Reardon*
George Cooper	*Fred Barden*
Tom Keene (as Richard Powers)	*Ted Elser*
Bud Osborne	*Cap Willis*
Zon Murray	*Nels Titterton*

Robert Bray	*Bart Daniels*
Erville Anderson	*Sethmier—the Liveryman*
Ruth Brennan	*Townswoman/Rider*
Harry Carey Jr.	*Cowboy*
Iron Eyes Cody	*Toma*
Ben Corbett	*Mitch Moten*
Joe Devlin	*Barney—Bartender*
Al Ferguson	*Chet Avery*
Clem Fuller	*Cowhand*
Robert Malcolm	*Sheriff Manker*
Ted Mapes	*Cowboy*
Chris-Pin Martin	*Commissary Bartender*
Al Murphy	*Cowboy*
Hal Taliaferro	*Cowboy*

The rights and materials for *Blood on the Moon* are owned by Warner Bros. along with most of the RKO film library. A Blu-ray disc of the film in NTSC format with subtitles sourced from the original camera negative was released by the Warner Archive Collection on April 28, 2020.

1. | The Author

When Frederick Dilley Glidden submitted his story "Six-Gun Lawyer" to *Western Story* magazine in 1935, the pulp magazine's publisher said the name of F. D. Glidden "didn't sound very western."[1] On the recommendation of his literary agent Marguerite Harper, Glidden adopted the more robust pseudonym Luke Short for *Blood on the Moon*. At the time, neither Glidden nor Harper realized the nom de plume was the moniker of a notorious Old West gunfighter. The actual Luke Short was a gunslinger, gambler, and army scout who was a friend of Bat Masterson and Wyatt Earp. Nevertheless, the name stuck. Fred Glidden, under the name Luke Short, would become one of the most prolific writers of Western fiction.

Glidden was born in 1908 in Kewanee, Illinois. His father, a well-to-do factory owner, died when his son was thirteen years old. Glidden was raised primarily by his mother, Fannie, a high school English teacher who eventually became dean of women at Knox College in Galesburg, Illinois. Glidden graduated from the University of Missouri in 1930 with a degree in journalism. According to the *Missouri Alumnus* of September 1931, Glidden and Edwin Hough, a fellow Mizzou graduate, "left New York on July 12 for an expedition in Northern Canada where they will spend

Frederick Dilley Glidden, aka Luke Short (courtesy of Aspen Historical Society; all rights reserved).

the year hunting, trapping, exploring, studying and writing."[2] The young man's appreciation for the rugged wilderness was whetted during an odyssey begun "from the northernmost terminal of the Canadian National Railways-Waterways [where] the boys embarked in canoes for a 75-mile trip down the Clearwater River."[3]

Glidden followed his Canadian sojourn with several brief stints as a newspaper writer. He eventually gave it up as a bad job: "I've read or heard that all newspapermen are disappointed writers, but in me you behold a writer who is a disappointed newspaperman. I've been fired from more newspapers than I like to remember, even if I could."[4] He relocated to Santa Fe, New Mexico, working as an archaeologist's assistant, and began writing stories about the Northwest. Glidden switched to writing Western fiction at the recommendation of Harper, who realized Canadian stories wouldn't sell well in the United States. He began his career as a professional fiction writer when *Adventure* magazine serialized his novel *The Feud at Single Shot* in 1936.

Pulp magazines had evolved from the dime novels of the 1800s. An 1896 issue of *Argosy* was the de facto starting point of the pulp era. By the 1920s, a plethora of genre magazines specialized in serialized Western, detective, mystery, adventure, horror, and similar stories. The Western-themed pulps, including *Adventure, Western Story, Blue Ribbon Western,*

Real Western, and *Frontier Stories*, paid their writers pennies a word. Glidden, Max Brand, Walt Coburn, and other Western scribes had to write constantly to make a living. After publishing his first novel, *The Feud at Single Shot*, Glidden became incredibly prolific, writing sixteen novels and hundreds of short and serialized Western stories. By the 1940s, he had moved up to writing serialized stories for the "slicks"—*Collier's* and the *Saturday Evening Post*—as prestige houses like Doubleday began to publish his novels. Writing about the West became a family enterprise: Glidden persuaded his wife to scribe Western romances, and his brother Jonathan wrote oater tales under the pen name Peter Dawson—his favorite brand of whiskey. Glidden was influenced by writer Ernest Haycox's (*Stagecoach*, *Union Pacific*, *Canyon Passage*) sense of place and ability to turn a phrase, but he exceeded Haycox—who died prematurely in 1950—in terms of plot design and character development. The acclaimed novelist Brian Garfield (*Hopscotch*) admired Glidden tremendously and credits the older man with influencing his work:

> I met Fred ("Luke Short") Glidden in 1955 or thereabouts. He was mayor of Aspen, Colorado, at the time and had a great office above the Post Office. He lived out in the woods on a very steep slope that overhung a river, and he could drop a fishing line from the porch right into the river. He loved to fish, but they had a home in Arizona, too. He was a big man, kind and gentle. Even though I was a snotty teen-ager, he treated me as a guy rather than as a kid, and he was generous enough to criticize a few short stories I had written. The most valuable advice he gave me over the next few years was, "Take out all the Western trappings. Your story should depend on characters and behavior. If it still works after you get rid of the clichés, it's a story."[5]

Despite sporadic forays into screenwriting, Glidden would stick mostly to penning Western fiction for the rest of his life. Based on Glidden's writing style, there wasn't an inordinate amount of difference between the two narrative forms; most of his novels were tailor-made for the screen. Glidden's dialogue and story construction lent themselves to adaptation into the three-act script format that has long governed Hollywood filmmaking. His novels were adapted for eleven different Westerns: *Ramrod* (1947), *Albuquerque* (1948), *Coroner Creek* (1948), *Station West* (1948), *Blood on the Moon* (1948), *Ambush* (1950), *Vengeance Valley* (1951), *Silver City* (1951), *Ride the Man Down* (1952), *Hell's Outpost* (1954), and *The Hangman* (1959). Glidden's dialogue was often used verbatim or simply repurposed by a legion of different screenwriters who condensed his stories to conform with film running times. Glidden's often graphic depictions of violence were either diluted or omitted entirely to comply with the edicts of the 1930 Production Code. He created realistic characters forged by the rugged environment of the West while melding them to interwoven plot elements that advanced his storylines. The fulcrums were often strong females, such as Amy Lufton in *Blood on the Moon*. This narrative trait is attributed to the strong influence of Glidden's mother during his formative years. Glidden's female characters could be misguided or disreputable but never tawdry—another reason his work was so readily adaptable to the screen. In *Blood on the Moon*, the relationship between Carol Lufton and Tate Riling leaves little doubt of its sexual dimension, even though there was nothing overtly salacious in the script due to PCA censorship restrictions. Glidden's intimate relationships between men and women stuck pretty much to the romantic perspective—in step with the times—unless the male character was a predatory villain.

Glidden's work would be treated both well and indifferently by

Hollywood. *Blood on the Moon, Station West, Ramrod,* and *Coroner Creek* are the best screen adaptations of his novels. They are also among the most noir-influenced of his stories. As Bertrand Tavernier observed, "The whole opening of [*Station West*] would hold a candle to any RKO noir of the period."[6] Other stories did not fare as well on screen. His engaging narrative of *Vengeance Valley* suffered in its film adaptation primarily because of the uninspired direction of Richard Thorpe and the miscasting of Robert Walker. *Albuquerque* and *Ride the Man Down* are no more than solid B Westerns, and *The Hangman* exudes the production values of a *Bonanza* episode, as an aging Robert Taylor is directed by an even older and ill Michael Curtiz.

Fred Glidden's ambition to write for the movies was nurtured by a duo of literary agents. New York–based Marguerite Harper was a tireless advocate of his work. Her voluminous correspondence with the author shows her to be consistently supportive while never failing to cajole him about progressing on different projects. She also offered her unvarnished opinions on both the quality and commercial viability of his writing. Glidden remained with the transparently honest Harper for thirty-two years. More germane to his movie work was Glidden and Harper's association with the legendary Hollywood literary agent H. N. Swanson. A young pulp writer who founded the periodical *College Humor,* Swanson arrived in Los Angeles when Hollywood Boulevard was a dirt road. After spending time as an associate producer at RKO, he opened his Sunset Boulevard literary agency in 1934. He was known to all as Swanie, and his client list became a veritable Who's Who of American literature: Ernest Hemingway, F. Scott Fitzgerald, Raymond Chandler, H. L. Mencken, James M. Cain, W. R. Burnett, Cornell Woolrich, and Elmore Leonard, among others. Swanson's guiding principles were patience and integrity, and since he thoroughly understood the film business and knew everyone in town who mattered, his agency set realistic expectations while negotiating to make its clients the maximum amount of money possible. During his storied six-decade career, Swanson became much more than a mere literary agent: he was a friend and mentor to those he represented.

2. | Book to Film

Fred Glidden's entrée into the movies was an object lesson about the challenges faced by a writer without screen experience attempting to gain an initial toehold at a Hollywood studio. *Blood on the Moon* was published as *Gunman's Chance* by Doubleday in 1941 and was sold to the *Saturday Evening Post* for serialization. After numerous rejections by other studios, RKO evinced interest but was not prepared to line the author's pockets with Tinseltown lucre. Marguerite Harper wrote to Glidden about the sale of *Blood on the Moon* to RKO on May 23, 1941:

> I had a long talk with Swanson when he was here a month ago—about which I will tell you later. . . . In any case he has an offer of $3500 for *Blood on the Moon* from RKO. I have told him to accept it. He is trying to sell it along with a service deal for you. I have said you would accept a stipend of four hundred per week for a several weeks contract. This might run four to eight weeks if he *can* sell your services to them to do work on *Blood* on adapting. All such contracts have options which would give us a chance to raise the ante definitely if the option was taken up. But it is essentially an easy way to find out how you like the work and how you feel about it. These movie decisions are apt to

Fred Glidden lights up a cigarette—the twentieth-century's screenwriter's companion. He ardently wanted to break into Hollywood screenwriting but not for short money (courtesy of Aspen Historical Society; all rights reserved).

> happen pronto such as wire saying: be here in 48 or 60 hours or a week or something. So, stay put or at least let me know where I can get to you by wire any time up to the second of June. As to the price, it is low, that we know. . . . Further on this movie business and my dealings with Swanson. We are splitting a ten percent commission—5% each way—so that any higher amounts are null and void. So, you can count on that for everything henceforth in the way of motion picture dealings.

Not hearing back from Glidden right away, Harper wrote to him again on May 28. Sensing that her client was unhappy about RKO's short money offer, she provided further insight:

> Swanson has been holding off trying to get at least 7500 for it and the story has had about 28 rejections I understand including producers who were individually approached. None of them thought very well about the story but considered it because of the Post tag to it. I personally can't see a good movie in it at all. Finally, everything else failing, Swanson got RKO to offer 3500 for this story as a "B" picture which means not their first and best output. . . . All the things you can argue about this I agree to. Small price, etc. etc. We can refuse to sell if you want to do so. The decision is yours. But it did seem like a good chance

> to get you there—which seems of some importance in view of your own desire to go.[1]

Wanting to break into movies, Glidden accepted a deal that paid him the most amount of money. In addition to a $2,500 flat fee for his story, he was also hired by RKO to adapt *Blood on the Moon* into a screenplay at $500 per week for three weeks. The intention was for the author to knock together an adapted script for the production of a B Western. Glidden wrote his initial draft of *Blood on the Moon* on March 14, 1941, followed by a second version dated July 9, 1941. Both scripts were slightly abbreviated duplications of his novel with little consideration made for adaptation to the screen. Writing cogent screenplays is a distinct skill set that many estimable authors, including James M. Cain and William Faulkner, never effectively mastered. At 260 pages, Glidden's script was long enough for a four-hour movie—a clear indication that he was not ready to fly solo. It dawned on RKO that the first-timer might need some help. The studio brought in veteran screenwriter Harold Shumate to rework Glidden's scripts.

Shumate was an experienced hack who had been writing original stories and scripts in Hollywood since 1917. His long résumé of films consisted entirely of B programmers, including *Hold Your Man*, *Girl in Danger*, *Parole Racket*, and *Konga, the Wild Stallion*. Shumate rewrote Glidden's script as a first-draft continuity on September 9, 1941. Although both men's names are listed on the cover page as "Story by Luke Short, Screenplay by Harold Shumate and Luke Short," the treatment is appended in the top left-hand corner of the first page: "Dictated by: Harold Shumate to Irene Voight. Started August 1, 1941." The probability of a production slate ever cracking on *Blood on the Moon* was seriously marginalized by the quality of a follow-on Shumate script titled *Gunfighter,* "based on the novel by Luke Short," dated September 30, 1941.

Shumate's *Gunfighter* screenplay changed Glidden's original story significantly, and not for the better. Although reduced to a more manageable 156 pages of standard scene settings, prescribed camera movements, fade-ins, and dissolves, *Gunfighter* replaced much of Glidden's crisp dialogue with pedestrian line readings that could have been borrowed from any of the nondescript B oaters ground out by Shumate. *Gunfighter* opens at the Ute agency with the Pindalest character rejecting Lufton's beef. This is followed by the meaningless insertion of ancillary characters at the Blockhouse Ranch who periodically wander in and out of the story at irrelevant times. Jim Garry's character is devolved into a not-so-bright saddle tramp who woos Amy Lofton with hackneyed dialogue ("Do calves follow you?").[2] The dramatic fight between Garry and Riling in the commissary saloon ends on a false note when Shumate has the hired gunslinger Reardon knocked unconscious by an umbrella. The *Gunfighter* script concludes with a desultory shoot-out at the Sundust jail involving the sheriff, Garry, and Amy Lofton versus Riling and several Shumate-created characters.

Since Glidden's initial script was essentially a condensation of his novel and the draft continuity and *Gunfighter* screenplays bearing Shumate's name didn't pass muster with Lee Marcus, the head of RKO's B unit, the three scripts were tossed onto the ever-growing stacks of unproduced properties that accumulated at Hollywood studios like raked-up piles of autumn leaves. The movie adaptation of *Blood on the Moon* was unofficially dead on arrival. Not surprisingly, nobody at RKO bothered to convey this fact to Glidden or his representatives.

Glidden's future in motion pictures appeared to be similarly bleak. He didn't want to relocate to Hollywood and refused to work for short money. He turned down subsequent offers in late 1941 from 20th Century Fox to adapt Ernest Haycox's *Sundown Jim* for the screen and from Harry Joe Brown at Columbia for something called *Pioneers*. Both studios refused to pay him more than RKO did for *Blood on the Moon*. It was left to Swanson to explain the realities of the movie business to Marguerite Harper in a New Year's Eve 1941 letter:

> Fred told us to tell Columbia he would not do it for less than $750 weekly. This killed the deal because they refused to better a "last salary." I even told Doran, scenario editor there, that they let us bring Fred an offer of a flat deal in which he be paid $750 weekly to establish the salary but to give them free time . . . so that he would not cost them over an average weekly salary of $600. Even this they turned down. Max Brand got the job yesterday. His established salary is higher than Fred's—I think it is $1000 weekly. He has been at Metro for three years and has eight screen credits including the successful "Destry Rides Again." I cite all this to show that Fred might be able to write rings around Brand, might even be twice as important in the magazine field as Brand. But from the producers' point of view, Fred has not yet learned his trade, has not enough credits on released pictures so that a producer could limit his risk and know exactly what he would be getting. . . . I'm not losing faith in him but merely trying to explain that Fred has *not* yet "proved himself" in Hollywood is so far as producers are concerned. They don't care if Fred makes two hundred thousand a year elsewhere. There's no reason for them to try and match his income. If he chooses to work in their medium, he must be willing to buck his salary and credits against other writers who are up for the same job.[3]

Swanson went on to say he was very enthusiastic about Glidden's new *Saturday Evening Post* story, "Ride the Man Down," but didn't think he could get him more than $500 weekly "since Blood on the Moon isn't even in production." The literary agent proved to be prophetic, as an unsigned Glidden letter to the agent caustically reveals: "Dear Swanie, Sorry about the news on *Ride the Man Down*. Tell those bastards for $750 a week I'll even write a Jap spy into the script. . . . It doesn't matter, because judging from the pictures I've been seeing they can't be paying money for them."[4]

While Glidden waited for his draft board to call him up for the war, he resolved to continue writing Western stories and no longer worry about the movies. The studios could come to him if they were so inclined.

3. | RKO Pictures

Considering Fred Glidden's inexperience as a screenwriter and the studio's own checkered history, having *Blood on the Moon* adapted into a credible film by RKO Pictures was, viewed retrospectively, a problematic venture. RKO's reputation as Hollywood's most indifferently managed movie studio was not entirely undeserved.

Since the 1931 merger of Joseph P. Kennedy's Film Booking Offices (FBO), the Keith-Albee-Orpheum theater chain, and Pathé Studios in Culver City under the umbrella of David Sarnoff's RCA Corporation, what was initially called Radio Pictures had been operated by a revolving door executive suite. Originally created to exploit RCA's Photophone sound-on-film technology, the studio spent most of its early existence struggling for financial survival. Despite Sarnoff's rapacious acquisition of movie theaters and the sporadic brilliance of successive production chiefs—beginning with William Le Baron (*Rio Rita, Cimarron*), followed by David O. Selznick (*What Price Hollywood?, A Bill of Divorcement, Topaze, King Kong*), Merian C. Cooper (who codirected *Kong* and produced *Little Women, Morning Glory*, and *Flying Down to Rio*), and Pandro S. Berman (*The Gay Divorcee, Alice Adams, The Hunchback of Notre Dame, Gunga Din*)—there was no consistent artistic and commercial vision from the top of the organization. It can be argued that RKO's diffused management engendered greater creative

RKO Pictures studio building on Gower and Melrose circa 1940. Rank-and-file RKO employees thrived under the studio's collegial working atmosphere, despite an executive suite revolving door (author's collection).

freedom to its filmmakers. But the long-term viability of a Hollywood studio was dependent on the consistent commercial appeal of its product along with the business expertise to produce, distribute, and exhibit its films.

Buffeted by the twin forces of rotisserie management and the Great Depression, the studio severely cut staff and filed for bankruptcy in 1933. Despite the continuance of managerial musical chairs amid more cost-cutting and consolidation, the studio now known as RKO Pictures clawed its way back. Its distribution of Walt Disney's monstrous hit *Snow White and the Seven Dwarfs* (1937) and the smashing success of the Fred Astaire–Ginger Rogers musicals buoyed the bottom line. By January 1940 there was cause for optimism. RKO emerged from seven years of receivership with little debt and $8 million in the bank.

RKO production chief George Schaefer (left) and producer Pandro Berman. Schaefer is best remembered for hiring Orson Welles and championing *Citizen Kane* before being cashiered for nearly bankrupting the studio. Conversely, Pan Berman enjoyed a long career as a successful film producer at RKO and MGM (author's collection).

In 1938 Sarnoff brought in George J. Schaefer from United Artists to run RKO. The brilliance of their 1939 slate (*The Hunchback of Notre Dame, Bachelor Mother, Fifth Avenue Girl, Love Affair,* and *Five Came Back*) was offset by fierce competition with the other studios as the "biggest little major" booked a slight loss.[1] Matters went rapidly downhill from there. Schaefer meddled in creative decisions as he attempted to run RKO much as the iron-fisted Harry Cohn micromanaged Columbia Pictures. But unlike Cohn, Schaefer lacked the essential attributes of a successful film mogul: commercial movie acumen, utter ruthlessness, and, most important, ownership of the studio. By the time Glidden was hired to write *Blood on the Moon,* George Schaefer had already made a pair of disastrous executive decisions: hitching RKO's future to Orson Welles and improbably hiring MPPDA censor Joseph I. Breen—who knew nothing about making movies save what should not be in them—as studio production chief.

Schaefer also accelerated the speed of RKO's management carousel. In addition to his bizarre selection of Breen, Schaefer replaced Lee Marcus as the B unit head, the vice president in charge of the studio resigned, a new executive producer of A films was hired, and a much-ballyhooed distribution agreement with Samuel Goldwyn was formalized. Unfortunately, Schaefer's ineptitude left Goldwyn in the driver's seat with overly generous terms. It soon became evident RKO couldn't make any money distributing Goldwyn's prestigious films. As talent exited owing to the war or fatigue from the RKO merry-go-round, Schaefer signed Broadway producer Jed Harris, director William Dieterle, and producer Gabriel Pascal to contracts, along with the European actresses Signe Hasso and Michèle Morgan. Most of these deals created nothing besides financial hardship; Harris and Pascal didn't make a single film at RKO before they departed the following year.

The September 1941 release of *Citizen Kane* should have been a triumph for Schaefer and Orson Welles. Instead, the film was sabotaged by the powerful Hearst newspaper chain, which decried Welles's fictional Charles Foster Kane's similarity to the lord of the yellow press, William Randolph Hearst. In addition to the Kane comparison, the similarity of Kane's second wife, played by Dorothy Comingore, to Hearst's longtime lover Marion Davies infuriated the venerable press lord. Despite some wonderful reviews, the unremitting war against the picture waged by Hearst's various factotums and newspapers scared off distributors. Cowed Hollywood studio heads attempted to buy *Citizen Kane*'s negative from RKO so they could destroy it. Despite Schaefer and Welles's admirable determination to release the picture, *Kane* lost more than $120,000 during its first run. By 1942 RKO was hemorrhaging red ink and bankruptcy loomed again. George Schaefer resigned in June, and Charles Koerner, head of the RKO theater chain, was appointed by Chairman Floyd Odlum to run studio operations.

4. | The Director

During the first decade of RKO's checkered history, Robert Wise was the model organization man. Born in Winchester, Indiana, in 1914, he spent a good deal of his youth obsessively watching movies in a trio of local theaters. Unable to continue in college because of the Depression-era collapse of his father's meat-packing business, the twenty-year-old Wise followed his older brother, David, to Hollywood in 1933. The elder Wise had worked his way into a position in the RKO accounting department. David gave his younger brother a boost with several interviews, which resulted in a $25-per-week entry-level gig as a film porter in the editing department.[1] After a year of carrying film cans, Wise was promoted to be an assistant to sound effects editor T. K. Wood. On the commentary track for the 1990 *Blood on the Moon* laser disc, Wise recalled that one of his first jobs in the sound department was dubbing in the beeps emanating from the RKO radio tower logo that opened the studio's films.

The young apprentice earned his first screen credit for *A Trip through Fijiland* (1935). He and Wood added music and sound to unused South Seas second-unit footage originally shot for *King Kong* (1933), creating a ten-minute short that earned him a $500 bonus. Wise moved into film editing as an assistant to William Hamilton. Hamilton, a facile editor of the Astaire–Rogers musicals, along with *Cimarron, Stage Door,* and *Topaze,* took Wise under his professional wing. They shared credit for several of RKO's prestigious 1939 productions, including *The Hunchback of Notre Dame, Fifth Avenue Girl,* and *The Story of Irene and Vernon Castle.* Wise later said that his assignment under Hamilton was one of the luckiest breaks of his career:

> It was extremely difficult for an assistant to actually cut film—you usually had to wait four to five years to edit a feature. Editors guarded their position jealously. Billy Hamilton was a brilliant editor but a periodic alcoholic. When Jim Wilkinson, the head of the editing department, put me under Billy, he said, "Remember, you're Billy's assistant, not his nurse." Hamilton never drank on the job, but he would disappear for four or five days and then drag himself into work. The first time I set up reels of dailies for Billy to cut, he said to me, "Why don't you see if you can put this together." I was stunned. He mentored me and became my benefactor. I am forever thankful that I worked under such a generous man.

Establishing himself, Wise cut *Bachelor Mother; Dance, Girl, Dance;* and *All That Money Can Buy* (a.k.a. *The Devil and Daniel Webster*). He itched to direct, and Garson Kanin eventually allowed him to helm some second-unit shooting on *Bachelor Mother* (1939). But being handed a director's megaphone at RKO was a proposition of much longer duration.

RKO's senior management dysfunction apparently didn't bother Wise and most of the rank-and-file employees. "Back in those days, the studios were making fifty to sixty features a year," recalled Wise. "About forty of these would be B movies on modest budgets, some of them pretty good pictures. You were always working, everybody was working. It gave you incredible continuity. I spent the first fifteen years of my career at RKO and enjoyed it very much. It was a small studio with a family atmosphere and a great sense of warmth, not a big, impersonal place like MGM." The actress Barbara Hale, who was signed by Charles Koerner in 1943, remembered that RKO, with its many young actors under contract, was "like a big college."[2]

Orson Welles had taken Hollywood by storm after landing a rich contract from George Schaefer that included final cut on his RKO pictures—an unheard-of concession by a Hollywood studio of that era to any director, much less someone who hadn't yet learned the business end of a camera lens. An envious Hollywood sharpened its knives and waited to see what the Boy Wonder would do.

It certainly didn't hurt Wise's career when Welles chose him as his editor while shooting *Citizen Kane* during the summer of 1940. Wise remembered Jim Wilkinson sending him down to the *Kane* set to be interviewed by Welles after an older editor failed to impress the neophyte filmmaker. "They were filming the beach party scene where Kane is an old man—in fact, the first six weeks I worked with Orson he was made up as an old man!" Although the two men got along well, the twenty-five-year-old editor would be alternately exasperated and awed by the equally youthful Mercury Theatre wunderkind. "He [Welles] would do things that would make you want to quit and then come up with an idea that was so brilliant your mouth would drop open," remembered Wise.

Wise helped Welles create what would historically be considered the greatest film ever produced by a Hollywood studio. With his editing ability on full display—particularly during the opening newsreel sequence and the memorable Welles–Ruth Warrick breakfast scene—Wise was nominated for a Best Editing Oscar® for *Citizen Kane*.

The Welles–Wise follow-on collaboration was, to put it mildly, not nearly as career enhancing. Welles prevailed in an internal tug-of-war with director William Dieterle (who was making *Syncopation*) for Wise's services on *The Magnificent Ambersons* in 1942. Welles overextended himself with several other projects, including radio work and starring in and directing *Journey into Fear*. He eventually had to hand over the directorial reins on *Journey* to Norman Foster; the film was being shot at night to accommodate Welles's frenetic schedule. Postproduction on *Ambersons* was complicated by Welles accepting an invitation from Nelson Rockefeller to be a goodwill ambassador to South America. Welles convinced Schaefer to allow him to segue his diplomatic sojourn into a vaguely defined film production set in Rio. Wise met Welles in Miami before he left for Brazil as the pair worked on a preliminary cut of *Ambersons*. Wartime travel restrictions prevented Wise from going to South America to continue the process, so he and assistant Mark Robson sent Welles the rough cut and attempted to edit the film according to Welles's detailed instructions provided in telegrams and long-distance phone calls. The sneak previews of the 131-minute film in southern California were disastrous—patrons walked out and audience feedback was entirely negative. Wartime audiences were bored by Welles's adaptation of the Booth Tarkington story about an Indianapolis family at the turn of the century. Wise was ordered by RKO to edit *Ambersons* into a commercially viable film, which is what he did, including overseeing several continuity scenes after nearly fifty minutes had been lifted from the rough cut. Wise's eighty-eight-minute edited version of *Ambersons* was tentatively released and then pulled by RKO. The film lost $600,000. It is worth noting that the draconian *Ambersons* edits by Wise were ordered by none other than George Schaefer before he was forced out and replaced by Charles Koerner.

Koerner had been brought in to run RKO with the mandate to make profitable films. The new studio head had no patience with Welles, who was unfairly perceived as the instigator of Schaefer's worst excesses. *It's All True,* Welles's never-finished South American film, was canceled and he was fired. RKO's unedited rough print and the original negative of *Ambersons* were incinerated. The fate of *The Magnificent Ambersons* has been chronicled in extensive detail elsewhere; Orson Welles and his legion of adherents nursed an understandable animus over the butchering of his film. Robert Wise was caught in a brace of conflicting loyalties between Welles and RKO. He simply did the best he could. The rough cut of *The Magnificent Ambersons* that Wise shipped to Welles in Brazil remains the Holy Grail of lost films, still being hunted in South America in an eighty-year Ahab-like quest.

Determining the measure of Orson Welles's directorial influence on Robert Wise is a speculative exercise. According to Wise, it was less than presumed but not insignificant:

> There were a few things I'm sure I learned from him. One was to try and keep the energy level high, the movement forward in the telling of the story. The other was the use of deep-focus photography. I've shot many of my films, particularly in black and white, with wide-angle lenses so we could have somebody close in the foreground and still have things in the background in focus. I'm sure that came from Orson. And, even though I had been a sound effects and music editor, I think Orson increased my sense of what a soundtrack contributes to a picture, both in sound effects and in music. Having come from radio, that was something very important to Orson, and my knowledge in that area was certainly heightened by my working with him.[3]

Concerning Welles's legacy of unfinished films and missed opportunities, Wise believed the notion of a Hollywood cabal conspiring to prevent Welles from making movies to be an inaccurate assessment. "*Citizen Kane* was the only time I observed Orson totally focused on a single project. *Kane* was his whole life." He believed Welles's incandescent brilliance was dimmed by his subsequent "self-indulgence and lack of self-discipline."

It's become conventional wisdom that Wise and those closely associated with Welles who remained at RKO were subsequently punished by management with bad assignments. Although Mark Robson was quoted as saying this was so, Wise always denied it. He edited three features after the *Ambersons* debacle, including *The Fallen Sparrow* (1943), in which director Richard Wallace allowed Wise to direct an additional scene with John Garfield. His continued campaign to land a directorial opportunity finally paid off after he was assigned to work with the producer Val Lewton.

Lewton was a former story editor for David O. Selznick. His show business connections included his aunt, the pioneer silent actress Alla Nazimova. He was hired by Charles Koerner to produce a series of low-budget horror films that would complement RKO's *The Saint* and *The Falcon* B mystery movie series and compete with Universal for the horror audience. Koerner controlled the $150,000-per-picture budgets and assigned the film titles, which were mostly sensationalist clichés. Within those parameters, Lewton could produce the films however he wanted.

Far from the stereotypical fast-talking Hollywood producer, Val Lewton was a sensitive and literate man. He was a skilled novelist and screenwriter who was obsessive about imbuing quality into his films while not taking advantage of or abusing people in his production unit.

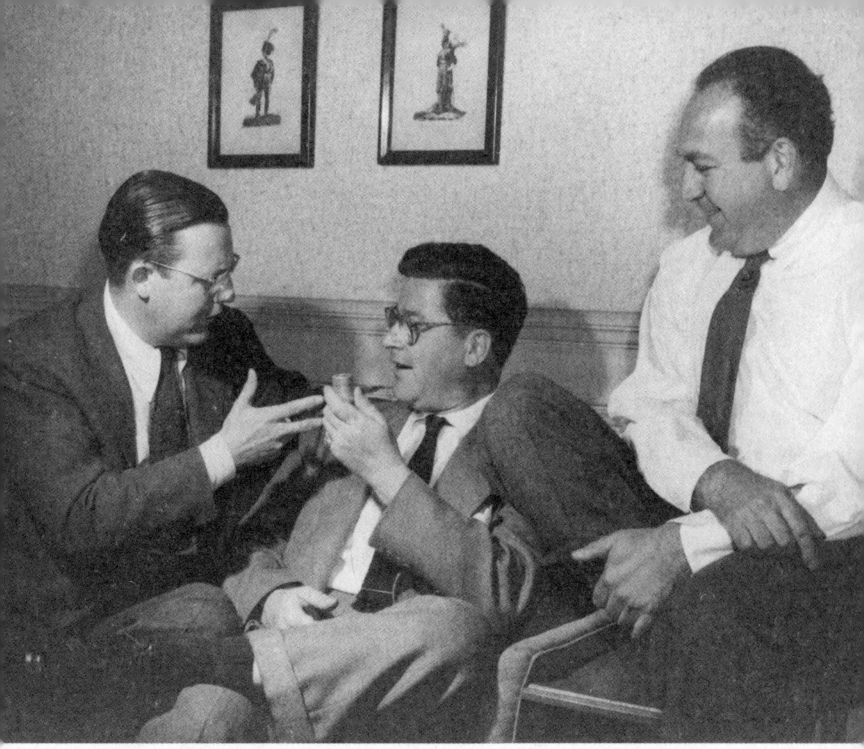

Robert Wise and Mark Robson with Val Lewton at RKO. An erudite man, too sensitive for the rough-and-tumble nature of studio politics, Lewton was an invaluable professional mentor for both young directors (author's collection).

Lewton loathed the ubiquitous studio politics and obligatory ass-kissing of members of the RKO executive suite, who would periodically offer up harebrained notions for his films that he had to pretend to consider. He functioned as the quarterback of a production team in which everyone at the table had a creative voice. Lewton's methodology would have a profound effect on the career of Robert Wise.

The spectacular box office results of *Cat People* (1942)—Lewton's initial RKO production reportedly grossed $2 million—gave him considerable breathing room with the studio brass. Not wanting his newly successful producer to get the prototypical swelled head and ask for more money, Koerner downplayed the success of *Cat People* by telling Lewton, "The only people who saw that film were Negroes and defense workers."[4]

Lewton produced a unique style of literate, successful pictures on lean budgets, including *I Walked with a Zombie* (a singular Caribbean slant on *Jane Eyre*), *The Leopard Man, The Seventh Victim,* and *The Ghost Ship* (both directed by Wise's editing colleague Mark Robson). He eventually succumbed to Koerner's insistence on a *Cat People* sequel luridly titled *The Curse of the Cat People*. Lewton wrote an imaginative story about a lonesome child with a fantasy friend who provides the love that she doesn't receive from her indifferent parents. To satisfy Koerner, he reused the cast of *Cat People*—Simone Simon as the friend; Kent Smith, Jane Randolph, and Elizabeth Russell—while stealthily calculating the studio chief wouldn't notice the sequel bore no resemblance to the original until it was already in the can.

Lewton assigned Gunther von Fritsch, who had previously helmed several RKO short documentaries, to direct *The Curse of the Cat People*. Von Fritsch was overwhelmed by his good fortune and quickly fell behind. Grossly overrunning schedule on a B movie put Lewton in an untenable situation: it was considered original sin by the rough-hewn RKO executive producer Sid Rogell.[5] It was von Fritsch's misfortune that gave Robert Wise his long-awaited opportunity to direct, as he related to Val Lewton's biographer, Joel Siegel:

> *The Curse of the Cat People* was to be his [von Fritsch's] first feature and I was the editor. A shooting schedule of eighteen days but he fell so far behind that after the eighteen days were used up, he was only halfway through the screenplay. Val tried and tried to get Gunther to pick up

the tempo, but it was his first big job and he was just too nervous to move any faster. One Saturday morning, I got a phone call from Sid Rogell, who was then head of the B-unit. I had done some second unit work for Rogell and had been after him to let me direct. Rogell told me I was to replace Gunther on Monday morning. Gunther and I had planned to do some extra night footage that very evening and I knew he had not yet been told of his dismissal. I couldn't bring myself to go to work with him under those conditions and called Val to ask him his advice. "Look," he said, "if it's not you, it will be somebody else. You're not pushing Gunther out." So I took over the picture on Monday morning and brought it in by early October. When I arrived on the set that first day, Val gave me a copy of Shaw's *The Art of Rehearsal* which I've kept with me ever since.[6]

Despite RKO's infantile promotion of "the sensational return of the Killer-Cat Woman," *The Curse of the Cat People* was hailed by no less than James Agee in *The Nation* as one of 1944's best films. Wise followed his debut by helming *Mademoiselle Fifi*, adapted from a Guy de Maupassant story set during the Franco-Prussian War. Since it wasn't a horror film, Rogell cut the film's already austere budget down to the bone. Saddled with rock-bottom production values, Lewton and Wise struggled to create a viable historical movie that was ultimately viewed as no more than a valiant effort. Matters would have been even worse had not Charles Koerner intervened on Lewton's behalf by removing him from Rogell's control and assigning him to executive producer Jack J. Gross.[7] Another studio bean counter whose idea of a creative horror film was, according to Mark Robson, "a werewolf chasing a girl up a tree," Gross produced *The Wolf Man* and *Son of Dracula* at Universal before landing at RKO. He was described in a personal letter from Lewton to his family as "an abysmally ignorant and stupid gentleman."[8]

Wise's next film for Lewton was a minor masterpiece. *The Body Snatcher* (1945) was adapted from a Robert Louis Stevenson story in the public domain about nineteenth-century Scottish grave robbers. British novelist Philip MacDonald and Lewton (under the pseudonym Carlos Keith) wrote an elegantly crafted screenplay outlining the ambiguities of good and evil. Boris Karloff starred as the ominous grave robber who provides a conflicted surgeon (Henry Daniell) with cadaver specimens for his medical school. Lewton's startling re-creation of 1831 Edinburgh was partially achieved by using the standing sets from *The Hunchback of Notre Dame* at the RKO ranch in Encino. *The Body Snatcher* is an exquisite, wonderfully made movie. Although Jack Gross forced the casting of an ill Bela Lugosi in a meaningless role for publicity purposes, for Wise the most memorable aspects of *The Body Snatcher* were the stellar performances of Karloff and Henry Daniell: "Because of the nature of the part and the duels he had with the doctor played by Henry Daniell, he put his heart and soul into it. I love those scenes between the two of them. Henry Daniell was a brilliant actor and Karloff knew it was going to be a challenge. I think he held his own with Daniell and did a marvelous job."[9]

A review of Robert Wise's working script of *The Body Snatcher*, which includes several interoffice communications from Val Lewton attached to the back pages, reflects the producer's influence on the young director, particularly in terms of wardrobe and set design, which he put to work in *Blood on the Moon* and his subsequent films. Lewton's September 11, 1944, interoffice communication to RKO's set designer Ben Piazza explaining his desired design of Henry Daniell's sitting room and medical school set reads like an extract from *Architectural Digest*:

> A Georgian room of ample and severe proportions, this chamber is nicely furnished with a Turkish carpet, Chippendale furniture of dark wood, framed engravings of great size, a pastoral in oil painting over the fireplace. The general effect is somewhat spoiled however by the fact that the room in always in considerable disorder; strewn with pipes, pipe spills, mugs, canes and other evidences of the fact that this is Bachelor Hall. An anatomical chart pinned to the wall, some surgical instruments strewn about, a shotgun and powder pouch in the corner and other odds and ends carry out the general impression we are trying to create.[10]

The Body Snatcher was Wise's last film for Val Lewton. Two months before the release of *Bedlam*, Lewton's final RKO production, Charles Koerner unexpectedly died of leukemia on February 2, 1946. Although RKO would enjoy the most profitable year in its history, Lewton had lost his protector. As his own health began to fail—he suffered the first of several heart attacks—Lewton left RKO for Paramount but couldn't get much going there. He later joined a production company with Wise and Robson that also didn't work out; the pair of former editors ended up replacing their old mentor, wounding him deeply. Lewton died of a heart attack in 1951 at the age of only forty-six. "The motion picture business literally killed Val," remarked a saddened Robert Wise.[11]

Wise settled in as a contract director at RKO with *A Game of Death* (1945) and *Criminal Court* (1946), a pair of mundane programmers. He had no choice but to helm these pictures, as he explained to author Sergio Leemann.

> When you're under contract like I was, you may turn down one or

> two films until they say, "Now come on, you have to do it." . . . They could lay you off for six weeks and would guarantee you forty weeks' pay but they could lay you off for up to twelve weeks without pay. So I had a period of eighteen weeks without income except my social security [unemployment insurance]. That's why I did films like *A Game of Death* and *Criminal Court*. Also, I was still learning. You don't learn when you're sitting at home. Everything you do should add to your repertoire, your knowledge of how to do things.[12]

Born to Kill (1947) appeared to be a harbinger of better things to come. Wise received a "nervous A" budget and a longer schedule to adapt James Gunn's lurid novel *Deadlier Than the Male* to the screen. The film featured an excellent cast headed by the fearsome Lawrence Tierney, the ace femme fatale Claire Trevor, and a delightfully sleazy Walter Slezak and is now acclaimed as the most visceral of films noir. Tierney and Trevor's romantic bonding, consecrated by animalistic lust and serial murder, revolted the period's critics. Bosley Crowther of the *New York Times* thought the film was "an hour and a half of ostentatious vice."[13] The film's publicity also suffered because of Tierney's drunken fisticuffs and a resultant Hollywood police blotter indicating his *Born to Kill* portrayal of serial killer Sam Wild might have been a semibiographical turn. Dore Schary, RKO's new head of production, was compelled to publicly distance the studio from its own film and star. Despite the critical brickbats, Wise knew the film had virtues. Nearly fifty years afterward, he said, "*Born to Kill* seems rather soft now. In terms of the dynamism of the story, however, it holds up well. I pushed very hard and was very instrumental in getting it done. I thought a lot of it was just excellent."[14]

Mystery in Mexico (1948) was a pleasurable experience for Wise. RKO owned nearly half of Churubusco Studio in Mexico City and believed producing a film using Churubusco's resources in Mexico might generate cost savings in Hollywood's increasingly dismal postwar fiscal climate. Wise made the film using Churubusco's entire staff amid constant haranguing from Rogell to reduce costs. The film turned out to be a mundane affair that didn't realize the studio any cost savings despite the RKO front office's economizing polemics. Wise, however, gained valuable expertise by living outside the country and working with a foreign crew on location for the first time.

5. |

Preproduction

Despite the collaborative atmosphere, Robert Wise was discouraged by the types of films he was directing at RKO. He realized depending on people like Sid Rogell to select his directorial assignments would consign him to B movie purgatory indefinitely. The director decided to search within the studio for a property he wanted to make and could convince the front office to get behind. Theron Warth was a close colleague from the editing department who shared Wise's ambition to ascend out of B movies. After cutting B features, including *The Mexican Spitfire's Baby* (1941) and *The Falcon and the Co-eds* (1943), Warth became associate producer of a pair of John Wayne pictures, *Tall in the Saddle* (1944) and *Back to Bataan* (1945). He shared the Best Documentary Oscar with Sid Rogell and the director Richard Fleischer for producing *Design for Death* in 1947.

After sifting through piles of unproduced screenplays in the RKO story department, Warth came across Glidden's book and the *Blood on the Moon* scripts. He and Wise read through all of them. Both men recognized Glidden's story as a viable film property that had been mishandled by RKO. The pair began working on the script and convinced Rogell to allow them to bring in screenwriter Lillie Hayward to compose a viable shooting script. If Hayward's script met with his approval, Rogell agreed to recommend green-lighting the film, with Wise directing and Warth producing.

Lillie Hayward was a pioneer female screenwriter about whom little is known beyond her extensive film résumé, which has been both overlooked and underappreciated. Born in 1889 in St. Paul, Minnesota, as Lillian Auen, Hayward was the daughter of Danish immigrants. She followed her sister Signe to Hollywood. As Seena Owen, Signe became a featured player under D. W. Griffith. After marrying cameraman Duke Hayward, Lillie began writing silent film scenarios in 1919 and sold her first script, *Janice Meredith*, in 1924. She enjoyed an extremely successful tenure at Warner Bros. writing pre-code staples, including *Frisco Jenny* (1932) and *Lady Killer* (1933), before going on to pen *Front Page Woman* (1935) and *The Walking Dead* (1936). *The Biscuit Eater* (1940), *My Friend Flicka* (1943), and *Black Beauty* (1946) were among her other credits before moving to RKO.

Hayward's track record garnered her the opportunity to produce *Banjo* (1947) at RKO. She adapted her original story and screenplay about a girl and her dog. It was a rare opportunity for Hayward at a time when the number of female producers in Hollywood could be counted on the remaining fingers of a mutilated hand. Unfortunately, despite being directed by the capable Richard Fleischer and having a solid cast, the picture didn't work out. It was previewed in front of a UCLA audience in Westwood, where the college kids booed the overtly sentimental family picture, threw concessions at the screen, and walked out. According to Fleischer, everyone involved with *Banjo* was subsequently fired, except him because he was under contract.

Despite the *Banjo* fiasco, Hayward remained a highly regarded screenwriter whom even Rogell respected. She was hired to write *Blood on the*

Moon at a total cost of $19,716.66. Hayward adapted Glidden's novel from his original draft and ignored most of Harold Shumate's changes and additional material. Much of Glidden's dialogue was appropriated as she trimmed all the fat from his narrative for the screen. The main omission was the character of Lufton ranch hand Ted Elser. In Glidden's book, Elser is obsessively in love with Carol Lufton and covers up for her when he learns of her affair with Tate Riling. This subplot was rightly viewed as superfluous and was omitted by Hayward. The Elser character, played by veteran Western actor Tom Keene, surfaces only briefly in a couple of scenes. The beginning of the film, when Lufton confronts Tate Riling at the Ute reservation, was dropped along with other extraneous scenes. Sequences certain to create censorship problems, including the Milo Sweet character being murdered with an ax by Tate Riling and one of the gunmen attempting to seduce the twelve-year-old daughter of a homesteader, were deleted.

RKO submitted the estimating script for *Blood on the Moon* to Joseph I. Breen (his brief hiatus at RKO had mercifully ended) at the PCA on December 17, 1947. The following day's response was from Stephen S. Jackson, a former justice of the New York Domestic Relations Court, who was being groomed as the replacement for an ailing Breen. Jackson reported that "the basic story seems to meet the requirements of Production Code," but he included several cautions about "no open-mouthed kissing" between the Tate Riling and Carol Lufton characters and warned that seven different scenes showing violence should be "shot in a manner that they will not be excessively gruesome."[1] He specifically requested elimination of a shot of Reardon kicking Jim Garry. The final revised script was submitted to Jackson by RKO on February 12, 1948. Jackson again requested dilution of "excessive gruesomeness" and any "passionate, lustful, or open-mouthed kissing." The censor specifically requested those scenes showing "Fred's horse dragging his lifeless body" and the stabbing of Jim Garry be minimized. Jackson took particular issue with the prolonged fight scene between Garry and Riling by devoting an entire paragraph to this "excessively long and entirely too brutal" scene.[2] He essentially dictated how to stage and film the entire fight to minimize the overt display of violence. Had all Jackson's recommendations been adopted, the sequence would have resembled a Three Stooges highlight reel rather than a life-and-death struggle between two desperate men. The combined skills of Robert Wise and director of photography Nicholas Musuraca in staging and filming this key sequence more or less intact while satisfying the censor's office remain emblematic of how period Hollywood filmmakers could bring realistic content to the screen despite the onerous Production Code restrictions they were saddled with.

Dore Schary's appointment as head of production in early 1947 initially boded well for RKO. Schary was a Broadway actor turned writer (he won an Oscar for cowriting *Boys Town* in 1938) who moved into producing for Selznick's Vanguard Films. His successful movies, including *I'll Be Seeing You, The Spiral Staircase, Till the End of Time, The Farmer's Daughter,* and *The Bachelor and the Bobby-Soxer,* were released through RKO. As production chief, Schary had his work cut out for him. The motion picture industry was entering a daunting era. Production costs had soared after World War II, with antitrust divestiture of studio theater chains and the blacklist and television soon to follow. Nonetheless, Schary was instrumental in ensuring *Blood on the Moon* would be a top-flight RKO production with Robert Wise at the helm.

Schary approved a budget of $1,289,811 ($939,681 of direct charges plus $350,130 of studio overhead). This was a full-fledged A-level movie by RKO in 1948. However, shortly before production began, Wise discovered he was being aced out of *Blood on the Moon* by his own agency. But Dore Schary, in addition to strongly supporting the film, prevented this particular double-cross:

> When I got my chance to direct, I signed the standard seven-year contract with RKO. My first picture starred Simone Simon and she was represented by Famous Artists [founded and run at that time by Charles Feldman, who branched out into motion picture production in 1945]. She talked to them and they approached me about handling me. I signed with them with the understanding that they would not take any commission from me, until I bettered my deal. That went on for a few years. They never did anything for me particularly, but that didn't bother me. We were getting *Blood on the Moon* ready for shooting when I got a call from Sid Rogell. He said, "You ought to check in on your agency. You got this project Dore Schary likes and wants to do, and they went up in the front office undercutting you, trying to sell another director and a couple of stars that they have." They were trying to make a package deal with James Stewart and somebody else, with Jacques Tourneur directing it. At that time Jacques was getting $75,000 a picture, big money. But Schary, who was then head of production at RKO, wouldn't hear of it. He said, "It's Wise's picture. He's been working on it, he's going to do it." That's the kind of man Dore Schary was—very straight, very honest. Of course, I left Famous Artists right away.[3]

6. | The Cast

Dore Schary believed James Stewart was too expensive for *Blood on the Moon*. Famous Artists then offered Jacques Tourneur and the already-contracted Robert Mitchum, pitching the duo as a reunion of the director and star of the recently released *Out of the Past*. Schary stuck by Wise but decided that this different type of Western would be a good turn for Mitchum, who had quietly become one of the studio's biggest male stars this side of Cary Grant.

Robert Mitchum was exactly the right actor to play Jim Garry. In 1937 the twenty-year-old Mitchum had hopped off an empty boxcar pulling into the downtown LA trainyard and shared a bottle of wine and a joint with a clutch of fellow hoboes huddled around a fire. This unheralded arrival parallels Garry's sodden entry in *Blood on the Moon* after he has lost his outfit to a stampede and is revived by some grub and coffee around Lufton's campfire.

Mitchum grew up poor and tough. When he was two years old, his father was crushed to death in a rail yard accident, leaving his twenty-five-year-old widow dead broke with two kids and another on the way. The family bounced around from Connecticut to New York's Hell's Kitchen trying to survive. At fifteen, Mitchum left home to tramp around the

Jim Garry (Robert Mitchum) didn't have much trouble keeping a corrupt Indian agent (Frank Faylen) under control (author's collection).

country; he became an authentic Wild Boy of the Road. Charged with vagrancy, he ended up on a chain gang in Georgia that almost cost him a leg before he began working reclamation for FDR's Civilian Conservation Corps (CCC). Southern California seemed a paradise after being on the bum during the Depression. The Mitchum family eventually settled in Long Beach. On a whim, Robert joined the Players Guild theater group and began appearing in local productions. Tall and imposing, he was an instinctive actor with great presence.

Westerns were the starting line for an actor who would have to pay his dues. Mitchum hired an agent named Paul Wilkins, who landed the neophyte an interview with Harry "Pop" Sherman, producer of the Hopalong Cassidy Westerns. Sherman hired the newcomer on the spot, while Sherman's assistant told the twenty-five-year-old thespian, "Don't shave."[1] The bestubbled Mitchum traveled to Kernville, California, the following day for his 1943 debut in *Border Patrol*, which was followed by *Hoppy Serves a Writ*, filmed in Lone Pine. He appeared in five other Hoppy oaters, mostly as a bad hombre.

Wilkins next got him a tryout at MGM, where the motto was "more stars than there are in heaven." According to Mitchum, director Mervyn LeRoy tested him at least thirty times before casting him in a key supporting role as Van Johnson's pilot buddy in *Thirty Seconds over Tokyo* (1944). After Metro dawdled about signing him to a contract to star in *The Robe*, RKO swooped in and inked Mitchum to a term deal beginning at $350 per week. The dubious payoff for ostensibly hitting the big time was a loan-out for *When Strangers Marry*, a King Brothers noir-stained cheapie filmed in a week at Monogram. Despite the pop-bottle budget, the picture garnered Mitchum critical praise and would be reissued shortly before the release of *Blood on the Moon* to capitalize on his stardom. Returning to RKO, he donned his Stetson for a forgettable Western comedy, *Girl Rush*, followed by a pair of more traditional oaters, *Nevada* and *West of the Pecos*.

Mitchum received the proverbial lucky career break after bumping into William "Wild Bill" Wellman on Vine Street. The iconoclastic director sensed the rangy actor was a fellow badass who would be perfect as the leader of Company C of the army's Eighteenth Infantry in what became *The Story of G.I. Joe* (1944). Mitchum's performance as Captain Bill Walker epitomized the somber reality of an American GI in close-quarters combat. Wellman strove for authenticity by using actual combat soldiers as background actors along with a cast of mostly unknown performers, headed by Burgess Meredith as the famed war correspondent Ernie Pyle. Mitchum's Oscar-nominated turn in *G.I. Joe* marked him as a rising star.

The success of *G.I. Joe* caused RKO to realize Mitchum could be as effective in uniform as he was wearing chaps. He starred opposite Guy Madison and Dorothy McGuire in *Till the End of Time* (1946), helmed by Edward Dmytryk. Like Robert Wise, Dmytryk was a former editor who had paid his dues during a stretch of servitude in the RKO B unit. He told Mitchum's biographer Lee Server that Mitchum "had the greatest photographic memory of any actor I ever worked with. If you changed lines, cut out lines, it didn't matter. He could adjust without hesitation. He was the most cooperative guy I've ever known."[2] Mitchum's recall was even more impressive to those familiar with his daily fortifications of booze and pot after a previous evening of pub crawling. The dichotomous nature of his personality reached full bloom with his rising stardom. Mitchum was an autodidact who sang and wrote poetry while mastering his craft as an actor. He also grew marijuana in his backyard and drank excessively while holding court in saloons with rowdy stuntmen. His stirring performance as a cowboy-soldier solidified his growing appeal, although *Till the End of Time* was overshadowed by *The Best Years of Our Lives*, a film that won eight Academy Awards in addressing the identical theme of returning WWII servicemen struggling to adjust to civilian life.

Mitchum's career continued its ascension primarily because of loan-outs. At MGM, a studio fumbling its way into the postwar movie environment, he appeared in the star-laden but muddled *Undercurrent* (1946), followed by *Desire Me*, a romantic misfire with Greer Garson shot in the first five months of 1946 and released in October 1947. Mitchum played his first legitimate romantic leading role at Warner Bros. in *Pursued* (1947), the previously mentioned Raoul Walsh picture that introduced Freudian

Jim Garry gets the drop on Tate Riling's men with a six-shooter in one hand and George Cooper in the other (author's collection).

film noir tropes into Westerns. He also appeared in Lewis Milestone's *The Red Pony* opposite Myrna Loy as a hired ranch hand who siphons away the affection of the owner's young son. Mitchum enjoyed working with Milestone while teasing the always poised Loy. But *The Red Pony* wasn't released until 1949, nearly two years after production wrapped, by which time much had changed for both Mitchum and RKO.

RKO's inability to cast Mitchum in an authentic starring vehicle with his name above the title ended with *Out of the Past* (1947). Now considered the apotheosis of classic film noir, the film features a hard-boiled script (honed to a razor's edge by Frank Fenton), aptly described by critic Roger Ebert as "an anthology of one-liners."[3] Aided by the peerless direction of

Jacques Tourneur and the shaded lensing of Nick Musuraca, Mitchum waded through a maze of vengeful heavies and double-crossing dames in creating an indelible persona of world-weary indifference that would stick to him like Krazy Glue.

Less than two months after *Out of the Past* wrapped, he acquiesced to sharing the screen as one of the three Roberts (with Robert Ryan and Robert Young) who adorned the social commentary success of *Crossfire* (1947). The film was a critical and box office smash—RKO's biggest hit of the year. Young got top billing and Ryan an Academy Award nomination; Mitchum was the overlooked third wheel. When he was featured with still-radiant Loretta Young and William Holden trying to shake loose his *Golden Boy* image in *Rachel and the Stranger* (1947), it seemed as though Mitchum was becoming a movie star in spite of rather than because of RKO. He had to settle for playing the discarded pioneer rival for Young's affections. It turned out that the second banana role didn't matter. By the time *Rachel and the Stranger* was released on October 2, 1948, everyone, including people who didn't go to the movies, knew who Robert Mitchum was.

Despite indifferent casting, Mitchum's work had more than outstripped his original RKO contract. His deal was reworked through a prototypical sleight-of-hand negotiation that jettisoned Paul Wilkins as his representative while making him considerably more money, a portion of which was shared with David O. Selznick's Vanguard Films. Mitchum's compensation for *Blood on the Moon* is listed as $121,954.70 on the film's production budget line. This sum reflected both his burgeoning status at RKO and what was being paid to Vanguard and Selznick for his services. Robert Mitchum was fast becoming a legitimate star.

As Jim Garry, Mitchum was aided by Lillie Hayward's *Blood on the*

Moon script, which played down the violent nature of his character as Glidden had originally created it. The novel portrays Garry as a taciturn, strong man with a sketchy past who eventually comes to terms with his conscience. The script leavens Garry into more of an itinerant stranger, a cowpuncher down on his uppers—and Mitchum's often bemused reactions accentuated this characterization. Hayward added an additional disclaimer when Garry says to Tate Riling, "This is the first time I've been hired for my gun."[4] Glidden's novel made it evident this was not the case. Wise enjoyed working with Mitchum and thought the actor was perfect as Jim Garry. "He just fit into the gear of it very well—his attitude and how he walked." The director described his star as totally professional and cooperative, although there was another element. "Mitchum was such a big, strong man," recalled Wise. "I always got a sense he was embarrassed to be an actor, as if it was sissified." The director added, "I'm sure he grew out of it." He also mentioned that Mitchum practiced assiduously with his six-shooter and was authentically "quick on the draw."

RKO had recently signed twenty-four-year-old Barbara Bel Geddes, who had established herself on the Broadway stage in *Deep Are the Roots* in 1946. Despite winning the Donaldson Award for her performance and being the daughter of famed stage and industrial designer Norman Bel Geddes, she left the Great White Way for Hollywood. "I remember Lillian Hellman and Elia Kazan telling me, 'Don't go, learn your craft.' But I loved films," she recalled.[5] Bel Geddes signed with RKO and made her screen debut with Henry Fonda in *The Long Night* (1947), a flop remake of the French film *Le jour se lève* (1939) that lost $1 million. *I Remember Mama* (1948), an acclaimed George Stevens drama about a Norwegian family in 1910 San Francisco, earned Bel Geddes an Oscar nomination for Best Supporting Actress. She was exactly the type of actress who appealed

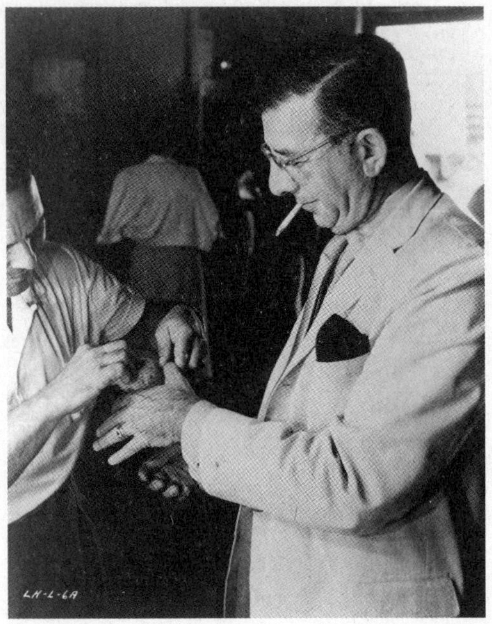

Dore Schary, the erudite RKO production chief, demonstrated integrity by insisting Robert Wise direct *Blood on the Moon* and resigning when Howard Hughes fired Barbara Bel Geddes and refused to produce *Battleground*. Conversely, Schary fired director Edward Dmytryk and producer Adrian Scott because of their politics and was a signatory to the notorious 1947 "Waldorf Statement" that codified blacklisting by the major movie studios (author's collection).

to Schary and Wise: a skilled thespian who was about craft, not glamour. Her character was tomboyish, but the sex appeal was nonetheless authentic. Wise described her as "feisty." The Amy Lufton character in *Blood on the Moon* is the spine of the story—loyal to her family, independent, tough, and wary of strangers, yet she ultimately convinces her father to trust the better angels of Jim Garry's nature.

Barbara Bel Geddes on location in Sedona. For her, firing blanks with a Winchester was easier than learning how to ride a horse (author's collection).

The Amy Lufton character is a direct contrast to her romantically deluded sister, Carol, played by Phyllis Thaxter, another actress with stage roots. Thaxter's role would be a departure from a career of being mostly pigeonholed as a devoted wife and "nice" woman, beginning with playing Van Johnson's spouse in *Thirty Seconds over Tokyo* (1943). Thaxter made her 1939 Broadway debut in *What a Life!* and understudied Dorothy McGuire in *Claudia*. When McGuire left to star in the Fox film version of the play in 1943, Thaxter toured with *Claudia* and was given a screen test and signed by MGM during the production's San Francisco run. She got a crack at an unusual role as a young woman with a split personality in *Bewitched* (1945), although her voice portraying the evil side of her personality was inexplicably dubbed by Audrey Totter. Following that was a series of supporting roles—in *Week-End at the Waldorf* (1945), as Spencer Tracy's daughter in *The Sea of Grass* (1947), and in *Living in a Big Way*

Robert Preston and Phyllis Thaxter were Blood on the Moon's star-crossed lovers (author's collection).

(1947). An added plus was Thaxter being a skilled rider of horses. Robert Wise praised the way she handled her scenes on horseback in *Blood on the Moon*.

In addition to casting Mitchum and Bel Geddes, Dore Schary decided Robert Preston was the optimal choice for Tate Riling, a devious, hail-fellow-well-met character. Preston had played a memorable Western heavy in *Union Pacific* (1939), along with appearing in a slew of notable films, including *Beau Geste* (1939), *North West Mounted Police* (1940), *This Gun for Hire* (1942), *Reap the Wild Wind* (1942), and *Wake Island* (1942). He was an excellent actor even if Hollywood never figured out how to tap his charismatic ability. "I played the lead in all the B-pictures and the villain in all the epics," was how Preston summarized his screen career.[6]

Actor Richard Erdman recalled Preston venting about his long-term contract with Paramount Pictures when they appeared together in *Wild Harvest* (1947): "They [Paramount] don't know what the fuck to do with me."[7] By this time he was making as much money as Alan Ladd (or more) and billed below him. Preston managed to terminate his twelve-year contractual run at Paramount in 1948 but would have to wait nearly a decade before he experienced a glorious second act on Broadway with *The Music Man*. Wise said that Preston and Mitchum were a simpatico team who worked well together and enjoyed playing practical jokes on Bel Geddes and Thaxter. Regarding their teasing of the actresses, Wise hastened to add, "There was nothing sexual or off-color about it. It was all in good fun."

Rounding out the supporting cast was an astute cadre of memorable character players.

Walter Brennan was already a legend in the movie business by 1948. The winner of three Academy Awards for Best Supporting Actor, Brennan was asked later in life how he gravitated to acting. He replied, "I got in it purely from hunger."[8] After losing all his money during a 1920s real estate bust, Brennan began at Universal by being able to imitate a donkey when the actual animal wouldn't bray on cue. Brennan and his wife grew their own vegetables and raised chickens at their San Fernando Valley home to feed their family while he embarked on a career as an extra. For many years it was a tough existence. Extras and bit players were paid little and were often treated no better than livestock until the passage of New Deal labor laws and recognition of the guilds. By the time Howard Hawks cast him as a miscreant in *Barbary Coast* (1935)—a role that allowed him to steal the picture—Brennan had already appeared in one hundred films and had either seen or done anything possible on a movie set.

Brennan's performance as the homesteader Kris Barden in *Blood on*

Walter Brennan as Kris Barden. A veteran of more than one hundred films, Brennan had seen or done everything possible on a movie set by the time he appeared in *Blood on the Moon* (author's collection).

the Moon is accentuated by his superb line readings. After eyeing Riling's "friends," who are hired gunslingers, he dryly observes, "I can buy that kind of friend for $75 a month and no questions asked."[9] Later, after his son is killed, he saves Garry from certain death by shooting Riling's gunman Reardon. When Garry asks why he rescued him, since they ostensibly are on opposite sides, Barden replies, "I always wanted to shoot one of you. He was handiest."

Wise related a story about Brennan and Mitchum whenever he was asked about *Blood on the Moon*. Mitchum's wardrobe and those of the film's other characters were made from sketches by ace designer and technical adviser Joe De Yong, who designed wardrobes for *Reap the Wild Wind*, *Shane*, *The Plainsman*, and *Buffalo Bill*, among other films. Wise told Mitchum's biographer Lee Server: "The first scene we shot after Mitch got outfitted was in the barroom. Walter Brennan was sitting at a table with a couple of pals and Brennan was very interested in the Old

West, it was a hobby of his. And I'll never forget when Bob came on the set, just standing there, with the costume and the whole attitude that he gave to it, and Brennan got a look at him and was terribly impressed. He pointed at Mitchum and said, 'That is the *goddamndest realest* cowboy I've ever seen!'"[10] In his *Blood on the Moon* laser disc commentary, Wise went out of his way to praise De Yong, giving him full credit for the authentic appearance of the film's actors: "He knew exactly how Western characters looked and dressed—he was brilliant. His work added significantly to the realism of the picture. I used him when I made my second Western, *Tribute to a Bad Man*."

Tom Tully played John Lufton with realistic panache. Tully, a former newspaperman who switched to treading the boards, struck the precise balance between a tough rancher willing to use deadly force to defend his livelihood and an honest John widower who has raised two daughters. His vigorous self-preservation and loyalty provide an interesting plot juxtaposition as he is hoodwinked by Riling through the betrayal of his daughter Carol.

Equally deft is Frank Faylen, whose turn as Jake Pindalest, the duplicitous Indian agent, is a double-edged portrait of deceit and cowardice. Faylen, at home playing easygoing characters or heavies, had received a career boost after his memorable turn as a sadistic alcoholic ward attendant in *The Lost Weekend* (1945).

Charles McGraw was well cast as the gruff, hot-tempered rancher with the memorable moniker of Milo Sweet. Decked out in a beard, a pair of six-guns, and a bearskin coat while chewing on a cigar, he was a veritable motif of a Western tough guy. Wise said the wardrobe perfectly matched the gruff character's demeanor: "Charlie McGraw—such a gravelly voice that fit that bearskin coat! That was De Yong's work!" McGraw arrived

Charles McGraw as Milo Sweet. McGraw's gravelly voice was a perfect match for his rugged appearance accentuated by a bearskin coat (author's collection).

in Hollywood in 1942 from the Group Theatre's cast of Golden Boy, in which he was billed as Charles Crisp. He quickly dropped his mother's surname, which in the film industry was associated with the actor Donald Crisp, and appropriated the more Irish-sounding McGraw. After his career was interrupted by the war, McGraw returned to Hollywood as one of *The Killers* (1946), a role that allowed him to quit his part-time job as a pin setter at Sunset Lanes. McGraw would make a splash as a murderous heavy in *The Threat* (1949), signing a seven-year contract with RKO in 1950.

Tom Tyler and Clifton Young rounded out the principals as Riling's hired gunslingers. A former stuntman, Tyler was a legend in the saddle, having performed in more than 140 Westerns since 1924. Young parlayed his career as a child thespian in the *Our Gang* comedy shorts during the 1920s into a solid run as a character actor that was tragically cut short when he perished in a 1951 Los Angeles hotel fire caused by smoking in bed.

The leading actors were selected by Dore Schary, but Wise cast all the supporting players and, perhaps most important, the film's director of photography. Born in Calabria, Italy, in 1892, Nicholas Musuraca had worked on the RKO lot since before the FBO era of Joseph Kennedy. Musuraca began as a chauffeur to the pioneer filmmaker J. Stuart Blackton. He eventually parlayed his fascination with photography into a job as a camera loader and operator on Blackton's films in the mid-1920s. He shot dozens of cheap Westerns and crime film quickies directed by low-budget workhorses like Lew Landers before finally graduating in 1939 to more prestigious pictures, such as *Five Came Back, Golden Boy,* and *A Bill of Divorcement* (1940). His reputation as a master of chiaroscuro lighting—frontal lighting and low-key lighting contrasted with high-key lighting and close shots—began with *Stranger on the Third Floor* (1940). RKO became the principal Hollywood studio on the front line of the postwar film noir movement primarily because of the stylistic work of Musuraca. Beginning in 1942, he successively lensed *Cat People, The Fallen Sparrow, The Seventh Victim, The Ghost Ship, The Curse of the Cat People, The Spiral Staircase, Deadline at Dawn, Bedlam, The Locket,* and *Out of the Past.* In addition to his impressive noir résumé, Musuraca excelled in other genres. He was nominated for a Best Cinematography Academy Award for *I Remember Mama* (1948); George Stevens's acclaimed sentimental drama wrapped three months before shooting started on *Blood on the Moon.*

A *Film Reference* article by Eric Schaefer analyzes Musuraca's unique photographic style:

> The whole of Musuraca's readily identifiable style can be broken down into five consistent fragments: the use of the complete tonal range of black and white; the low placement of lighting sources; narrow beams

Director of photography Nicholas Musaraca. His darkly stylistic camera work resulted in RKO Pictures being dubbed "the capital of noir." (Courtesy of American Society of Cinematographers)

of high-key light within a dark frame; a silhouetting technique with an emphasis on lighting for contour; and a penchant for abstraction. The first of these stylistic signatures is the use of the full tonal range of black and white. . . . His second rule provided a naturalistic means to achieve an expressionistic result. The low placement of light sources—often in the guise of table lamps, but also fireplaces and campfires—netted a highly expressionistic look as the illuminated subject was trapped by his or her own shadow looming on the walls and ceiling above. The creation of claustrophobia within the frame provided visual collusion for the onerousness of *film noir* narratives. The third Musuraca trait called for tightly defined high-key light focused on objects, most often faces, in the black void. The technique simultaneously directs the eye to the primary point of interest within the frame while emphasizing the surrounding darkness leading to a tension as the conflicting tones attempt to dominate. Musuraca's fourth and most readily identifiable trademark is a skimming-silhouetting technique. Figures or faces in

> the foreground are lit from the side or rear, emphasizing contour while leaving the front largely dark. The resulting highlighted contour of the silhouetted object separates it from the background adding depth to the frame.... A strong reliance on tonal tension featuring large areas of black led Musuraca to the verge of abstraction in many cases. This fifth trait is evident in a number of the films he photographed as the frame is shattered into geometric patterns of light and shadow."[11]

Wise selected Musuraca because he knew the cinematographer would provide the precise visual aspect he envisioned for *Blood on the Moon*. "There were a number of great photographers at RKO who shot in that dark, shaded style—Robert De Grasse and Russ Metty," remembered Wise. "But Nick Musuraca was the king of low-key lighting. I rarely used the same DOP twice, but I wanted Nick very much for this picture." As a director, Wise had worked with Musuraca once before on his very first picture, *The Curse of the Cat People* (1944), where he had replaced the originally assigned director and had no say about who would shoot it. However, he edited several of Musuraca's other films: *Bombardier* (1943), *The Fallen Sparrow* (1943), and *Marine Raiders* (1944). Musuraca possibly lensed several of the retakes Wise helmed for *The Magnificent Ambersons* (1942) in addition to his extensive editing of Welles's film. Wise was very familiar with Musuraca's work and knew it was exactly what he wanted for *Blood on the Moon*—a Western that would be shot in the film noir style.

7. | Production

The production of *Blood on the Moon* was scheduled for forty-eight days, starting February 15, 1948. According to Wise, the picture began production earlier than he desired because of "Robert Mitchum's commitments to other films." Because of the early start date, filming in Arizona would involve significant production problems. Wise completed photographic tests of the principal actors at RKO on February 12. A crew of fifty included Wise, Theron Warth, assistant director Maxwell Henry and six assistants, Nick Musuraca and seven other cameramen, two make-up artists, six electricians, eight soundmen, two wranglers, a transportation clerk, and the wardrobe, construction, and property crews, along with Robert Mitchum, Barbara Bel Geddes, and their stand-ins. All departed from RKO's Marathon Gate at six o'clock on the evening of February 14. A note on the morning's call sheet ominously cautioned, "Everybody prepare for cold weather."[1] The rest of the actors joined the company several days later at the Sedona Lodge.

The film's opening of Mitchum in a rainstorm was noted by Wise in his shooting script as "Nite, Dawn, Evening." The following close-in shot of the star was annotated as "Get Process CU," indicating that this was a process screen shot. Sets had been hurriedly built at specific locations to

The three Roberts of *Blood on the Moon*: Mitchum, Wise, and Preston (author's collection).

accentuate the photographic attributes of the Sedona Verde Valley's famous buttes. The biggest set, the Lufton ranch, consisted of a corral and several false-front buildings constructed on a plain opposite the Two Nuns rock formation in Little Horse Park. Other sets included the Ute reservation, the site of Agent Pindalest's office. The long shots of the reservation were given visual heft courtesy of a matte painting of a montage of Indian tepees. The Barden ranch house was a matte shot; the front of the house, the corral, and the interiors were filmed on RKO's Stage 10. Tate Riling's house was an existing cabin structure in Sedona dating to the 1920s. Historically called the Van Deren Cabin, it is actually two small structures with a connecting roof that still stand and are maintained by the US Forest Service. A plaque at the cabin commemorates its use in *Blood on the Moon*.

Immediately upon arrival, Wise had to cope with inclement weather. The original plan was to wrap up location shooting within a week and return to Hollywood. Although the budget was generous in comparison to RKO's customary parsimony for Westerns, this didn't allow much leeway, particularly for a director attempting to transition out of B films. Coming up under Val Lewton and working for unsentimental taskmasters like Sid Rogell, Wise was a fast worker who was adept at doing more with less. Aside from his craftsmanship, Bob Wise was also one of the kindest and most likable men in the business. The cast and crew wanted both him and the picture to make good. Even with that, the director's unruffled temperament would be sorely tested in Sedona.

The company settled in at the Sedona Lodge, followed by a nine o'clock call the next morning, February 16. After twenty minutes of rehearsal, shooting began at the river location for the initial confrontation between Mitchum and Bel Geddes. On this first day, the company lost two and a half hours because of lack of sunlight. Cloud cover moved fast in the Sedona Verde Valley and mixed rain- and snowstorms were frequent. Six hours were lost for the same reason on the following day; the RKO daily production report noted the company "rehearsed 4 of the 6 hours."[2]

The situation repeated itself every day. When Wise moved from the river to the Lufton ranch set, the lack of sunlight cost him another two and a half hours. On February 20, they lost only half an hour as Musuraca and Wise reviewed the shot list, moved reflectors around, and consulted weather reports in their attempts to wring efficiency from a situation they had no control over. On February 23, Wise attempted to film at the edge of the mesa, though the daily production report noted a "loss of 5 hrs. due to snow, sleet, hail, rain and overcast."[3] After losing a half day at the Indian agency set, they spent the rest of the day lining up matte shots.

They were completely rained out on February 25 and 26 and remained at the lodge. On the following day they returned to the Ute agency set. Despite heavy overcast that developed from light drizzle to snow, Wise and Musuraca decided to expose film anyway. The following day, at Riling's cabin, they were rained out. Wise later said he "tracked the weather like we were at NASA for a rocket launch." He tried to stay ahead of the rain, snow, and cloud cover by making decisions on where to shoot and quickly moving to other locations on the basis of weather reports. During his laser disc commentary, Wise remembered how challenging it was to film in Sedona during February and March 1948: "We used to chase the sun all over that valley. I received three daily weather reports: one from Los Angeles, another from the local airport, and one from Washington. These reports were never in agreement and they were never correct. It was a maddening problem." Despite the challenges of the weather, Wise and the company were entranced by the beauty of Sedona's red rock cliffs. The director admitted, "Sometimes we regretted not shooting in color."

In an attempt to speed things up, Wise divided the company into two units on March 1. The second unit, headed by producer Theron Warth, shot external footage of Riling's cabin and long shots of riders on the heights. For these, local wranglers provided upward of fourteen horses. Splitting the company and shooting with inadequate light saved time, and there was an additional attribute. As Wise specifically chose Musuraca for "that moody style" of a film noir, the cloudy weather tended to give the film a visual boost.[4] But heavy rain that intermittently turned into snow shut down filming completely on February 28 and 29.

Despite the difficulties, Wise persevered to get the needed footage, including shooting retakes of Mitchum on horseback when the cloud cover lifted. When the company was idled, they rehearsed on location

Barbara Bel Geddes tends to a wounded Mitchum while nursing her saddle sores off camera (author's collection).

or at the hotel. Bel Geddes was still learning how to ride horseback and endured an acutely sore behind during the Sedona shoot. Wise camouflaged her inexperience by using doubles whenever possible along with judicious camera angles and editing, such as cutting away to Mitchum when she was mounting her horse in one scene. One of the female riders doubling Bel Geddes and Thaxter was Walter Brennan's daughter, Ruth, who was an accomplished cowgirl.

Blessed with an amazing memory, Robert Mitchum required minimal rehearsal time. The actress Jane Greer recalled Mitchum arriving for a morning call during the shooting of *Out of the Past*, asking, "What are the lyrics today?"[5] A quick glance at the script and he was ready to go. Despite the short schedule in Sedona, there was still time for diversion.

Arizona State College at Flagstaff asked him to choose a coed to be the school's 1948 yearbook queen. Mitchum, "rated by feminine movie goers as the greatest heart throb that has happened to them since Clark Gable," according to the *Arizona Daily Sun*, initially demurred because of the problematic production schedule.[6] But in a break from the routine, he and wardrobe director Robert Richard, along with makeup man Webster Phillips, attended the La Cuesta A Club dance at Ashurst Auditorium on the evening of February 20, where he crowned a freshman, Patricia "Skip" Johnson, as queen. The arrival of his wife, Dorothy, at the Sedona Lodge on February 29 might have forestalled Mitchum from any further exploration of the college's coed scene.

Filming continued in Sedona until March 3, at which point the company packed up, returning to Hollywood the following day. Wise later said that the company had been snowed out and would have to use locations closer to Hollywood to finish the film. At this point, the production was six days behind. The short duration of this schedule lapse was close to miraculous considering the extreme challenges of the Arizona weather. The filming in Sedona comprised 156 camera setups for 91 different scenes that encompassed slightly less than sixteen minutes of the film's eventual eighty-eight-minute run time. Shooting recommenced on March 5 at RKO's Stage 6 on the interior set of Lufton's ranch kitchen with Mitchum and Bel Geddes.

On March 6 the company moved to the RKO ranch facility in Encino, where the scenes of Garry facing down gunmen Joe Shotten and Frank Reardon, who were attempting to murder John Lufton, were filmed. The RKO ranch, an eighty-nine-acre facility with a Western town set and a New York–style street, had been used for dozens of films, including *Cimarron*, *Bringing Up Baby*, *The Hunchback of Notre Dame*, *The*

Bellying up to the bar on the RKO lot. Left to right: Charles McGraw, Robert Mitchum, Robert Preston, Clifton Young, and Joe Devlin (author's collection).

Magnificent Ambersons, and *It's a Wonderful Life*. Howard Hughes eventually sold the facility to the city in 1954, and the land was converted into a housing development and a public park. Filming continued with a 10:00 a.m. call at RKO Stage 6, followed by an all-night shoot on the ranch's Western Street. In his shooting script, Wise chronicled Garry's entrance into Sundust at the RKO ranch for his initial encounter with Tate Riling and his group of agitated farmers, appending reminders about wardrobe: "Play Jim with sheepskin on again. Sweet's [Charles McGraw's] hat and fur coat. Riling, Shotten and Rearden outside coats. Homesteaders extras outside coats."[7]

These scenes included Garry being mistaken for Lufton's hired gun.

He spots Carol Lufton on horseback, throwing a rock with a message attached into Tate Riling's window as he is chased and shot at by Milo Sweet. Wise reveled in these night sequences, as they validated his vision for how *Blood on the Moon* should appear on screen: "That dark, moody, dramatic look was why we shot so much of the picture at night. It made it more dynamic in terms of mood and enhanced the story. It really paid off to shoot at night."

There were very few blue pages and annotated changes to Lillie Hayward's script beyond minor dialogue modifications, such as "back of the barn" altered to "back of the corral."[8] The final confrontation between Carol Lufton and Tate Riling swapped out a scripted stove for a fireplace, and Wise had Carol strike Tate Riling when the extent of his betrayal finally dawns on her.

Blood on the Moon presented Wise with an ample training ground for managing a cast, crews, and satellite units filming at multiple locations. Add to those challenges the fact that the director was working in a genre that, at least on paper, he was totally unfamiliar with. Wise stated in his commentary about the necessity of preproduction research: "Research is critical for a director. You have to immerse yourself in the truth of your subject—you read, check photographs, and study. You have to know what you put up on the screen is true."

The consummate technician, Wise worked extensively with art directors (Albert D'Agostino and Walter Keller as well as Joe De Yong. *Blood on the Moon* would be the last film Wise directed for which he didn't storyboard all his scenes. "I'd arrive on the set early, before anybody else, and examine it, walk around. I'd get in my mind the possible camera angles and shots that we would use before the rest of the crew arrived."

In addition to the location work in Arizona before the return to

Hollywood to film at the RKO ranch and studio sets, a number of scenes were shot at a cattle ranch in Castaic, California. Although Wise stated in his audio commentary that these scenes were shot in Calabasas, in the far northern end of the San Fernando Valley, this was a rare instance where his memory of events nearly a half a century earlier appears inaccurate. According to the film's production records, no portion of *Blood on the Moon* was filmed in Calabasas.

Located between Los Angeles and Bakersfield, near the Angeles National Forest, Castaic was certifiably rural in 1948. On March 25–27 an assistant, Edward Kelly, and a cameraman identified as "Wellman" filmed a cattle stampede at Lyons Ranch in Castaic using "100 cattle and 19 horses."[9] These shots included the sequence in which Fred Barden (George Cooper) is murdered and his body is dragged on the ground by his horse—the scene originally objected to by the PCA censor. The daily production report noted a problem with the dummy being pulled by the horse, which necessitated reshooting that portion of the scene. Wise also moved most of the company to Castaic to film scenes of the actors at the external line camp as the stampede occurs. These sequences included a $100 bit part by Harry Carey Jr., who is briefly glimpsed in a group shot staring at Fred Barden's corpse still attached to his horse's stirrup and murmuring a single line: "Just a month ago, he and I went to a shindig together." *Blood on the Moon* employed several riding doubles for the actors, including James Van Horn, the older brother of legendary stuntman Buddy Van Horn, who would direct several films for Clint Eastwood.

The production experienced a cost overrun of $3,533, as it took two extra days at Lyons Ranch because of a delay in transferring a portion of a set from Sedona. Wise also had to spend an evening filming at Iverson's Ranch, a venerable Western location northwest of Chatsworth near

Simi Valley, for shots of Mitchum, Brennan, Tyler, and Preston outside the commissary saloon.

On March 8 a small unit consisting of director Arthur Rosson, British-born cameraman Jack MacKenzie, and assistant Clifford Stine was sent from RKO to film in the mountains of Colorado to obtain "camp and trails" footage of Garry traversing the mountains to the Ute agency, inveigling Pindalest to return with him as Riling, Sweet, et al. searched for them.[10] The team traveled to Idaho Springs, in the mountains about thirty miles from Denver. Using six horses and several extras, the crew spent two weeks filming mountains, snow, and a lot of long shots of extras dressed to resemble Mitchum, Faylen, McGraw, Preston, and Espera Oscar de Corti, better known as Iron Eyes Cody. Cody was an actor of Italian heritage who enjoyed a lengthy career playing Native Americans in movies and later on television. (He identified with his screen image to the extent that he created a fictional lineage of a Native American, claiming membership in various tribes.) Despite a misdated *Variety* squib stating that Preston and McGraw were sent to Estes Park, Colorado, to shoot exteriors, there are no production records of any of the principal actors traveling and participating in the Colorado location scenes.

The Colorado footage would be astutely cut by editor Samuel Beetley using close-up shots of snowbound actors and Garry and Pindalest's mountain campsite, which were filmed on the Pathé lot process stage. The Pathé studio at Culver City had been owned by RKO since Joseph Kennedy purchased it and was leased to David O. Selznick, first as Selznick International Studios and after 1946 as Selznick's Vanguard Films. After the experience in Sedona, RKO didn't have the budget to spend any further time on location with a cast and crew. Wise had to rely on matching long action shots with medium shots and close-ups of the actors in front

RKO-Pathé Studios in Culver City, originally built by pioneer mogul Thomas Ince, was the site of *Blood on the Moon* interior scenes that matched the snowbound Colorado location footage (author's collection).

of a process screen, onto which scenes of snow and the cattle stampede were projected. A Moviola machine was used for the snow sequences. Wise ensured all of these sequences matched as closely as humanly possible.

On March 26 Wise staged and filmed the fight between Garry and Riling on RKO's Stage 5. It was his favorite scene in the picture. To begin with, he was happy with the configuration of the bar set. "I loved the low ceilings because it allowed interesting low camera angles," Wise remembered. "John Ford said, 'An eye-level camera is a dull camera,' and I agree with him." The director specifically wanted to avoid the clichéd Western saloon brawl featuring "a brigade of stuntmen falling over bars and crashing through windows." This scene was about "two men wanting to kill each other," both being beaten to a pulp and exhausted at the end. He

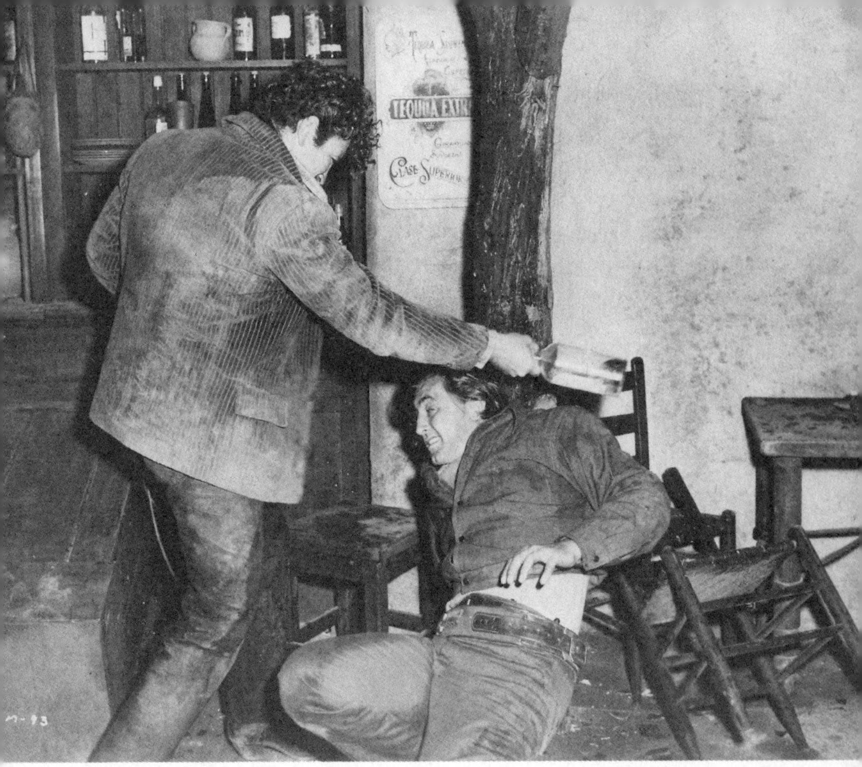

Preston versus Mitchum in *Blood on the Moon*'s no-holds-barred fight scene, meticulously choreographed by Robert Wise and filmed by Nicholas Musaraca (author's collection).

briefed Mitchum and Preston extensively on what he wanted, and they agreed enthusiastically with Wise's concept. The actors threw themselves into the scene, and their fight in the darkened saloon, which Musuraca seemingly lit with little more than birthday candles, is a masterpiece. Wise said he had a hard time convincing the stunt doubles (Carl Saxe and the renowned Gil Perkins) to limit their time in front of the camera; Preston and Mitchum performed most of the action themselves. Shooting on this sequence began at 9:00 a.m. and wrapped at 5:10 p.m. Wise was well satisfied: "I was particularly pleased with the fight because it came out the way I planned."

Theron Warth and a camera crew returned to Castaic. From April 8 to April 13 they filmed the nighttime cattle stampede through Garry's camp that opens the film. Wise's shooting script for these sequences is appended: "camera car shot, no cattle." For Lufton's riding and shooting to turn the herd, he wrote, "Possible double. Process shot." Production wrapped with process shots of the actors against the stampede footage using a mechanical horse borrowed from MGM. The final external sequences, "Jim's 2nd camp" and "Jim's first snow camp," were filmed on Pathé Stage 15 between April 15 and April 20. Several actors, including Frank Faylen and Charles McGraw, were brought back to complete these shots.[11] According to the final RKO production report of April 20, 1948, appended with the words "picture finished," *Blood on the Moon* tallied fifty-six days worked and four days of travel, finishing ten days behind schedule. The rough footage of ninety-seven minutes and forty-three seconds was ready for editing.

8. | Postproduction

Although he refrained from micromanaging editor Sam Beetley—"as a director you need the objective advice of a skilled editor"—Robert Wise closely oversaw the postproduction cutting of *Blood on the Moon*. As a former editor, Wise knew the importance of providing adequate material for the editor to work with, but he didn't get carried away. "I think the notion of shooting everything from every possible angle is ridiculous," he remarked during his commentary on the film. Wise also reminisced: "I remember editing Gregory La Cava on *Stage Door*. He had the least amount of coverage. You literally put the film together how he shot it, but it worked for him. Orson had full coverage—not overly done, but well done." Wise said the last bit of pure editing he did on any of his films was in *The Set-Up* (1949). The assigned editor couldn't cut the fight sequences between Robert Ryan and Hal Baylor to Wise's liking, so he took over and did it himself.

Wise apparently gave no consideration to revamping and reshooting what appeared to be a traditional ending to make it more melancholy or ambiguous. Lillie Hayward's script certainly had a more upbeat finale than Glidden's book, which depicted Jim Garry and Amy Lufton looking to their future together rather than heading into Kris Barden's house with Amy's father and the homesteaders for a premarital toast. The theme of redemption for the ambivalence of Jim Garry was orchestrated by Bel Geddes with one of the best lines in the film. When Garry returns to Lufton's ranch after the commissary fight with a cut hand, which is bandaged by Amy, he tells her father about the swindle set up by Riling and the Indian agent Pindalist, as well as his part in it. As he starts to leave, Amy halts him by saying, "You don't go tell a dead man he's dead. You came here for something else too."[1]

Amy then rides after Garry and attempts to convince him not to leave by explaining her father misunderstood his intent and believed Garry meant to kill Pindalist. She refuses to let him go while addressing his apparent moral incongruity: "I know you better than you think. You've been in hard luck and made mistakes . . . but you've never admitted them . . . except to yourself. . . . This mess with Riling . . . you never liked it . . . that's why you walked out on it." As Garry stares into the fire, she continues, "Today you tried to do something that would make up for it and Dad threw it back in your face. He thought you were proposing to kill Pindalist. I didn't think so. I know why you did it—you thought it would help wipe out the past." Garry nods mutely as she concludes, "You're proud, Jim, but this is the wrong kind of pride. If you ride on back to Texas, you're lost." The scene dissolves and the next shot has Garry on horseback crossing the Massacre River on his way to the Ute reservation to con Pindalist in order to give Lufton time to round up his cattle.

While this sequence was not nearly as clever as Mitchum double-crossing Jane Greer in *Out of the Past* and being gut-shot in the front seat of a station wagon for his trouble, it was good enough not to trifle with. The finale restored the traditional context of a Western, but the key discriminator in *Blood on the Moon* is less about what occurs and more about how and why. The breathtaking pictorial vistas of the Sedona Valley are ultimately uninspiring; they merely serve as a backdrop to a clutch of hardscrabble ranches and the barren town of Sundust, which consists of a pair of darkened saloons. Law enforcement is sketchy at best; the local sheriff (Robert Malcolm) is glimpsed in a brief scene kowtowing to a fulminating Milo Sweet (Charles McGraw). The region is replete with corruption, betrayal, greed, and desperation. There are no flashy heroes. Jim Garry is bereft of everything, save his gun and saddle. He is uncertain where his loyalties lie as he rides alone in the gloom. *Blood on the Moon* could have just as easily been filmed in an urban setting, which is exactly how Robert Wise envisioned it.

Blood on the Moon's score was composed by Roy Webb, RKO's chief music composer. A protean craftsman who scored more than 360 films, Webb has been historically overlooked and is often excluded from the renaissance of appreciation for the great twentieth-century film composers—including Max Steiner, Miklos Rozsa, Bernard Herrmann, Erich Wolfgang Korngold, Alfred Newman, and Dimitri Tiomkin. But his work was often just as distinguished as that of his more lauded contemporaries, and Webb was nominated seven times for the Best Music Academy Award. Roy Webb was born in New York in 1888, attended Columbia University (he composed the school's official football fight song, "Roar, Lion, Roar," in 1925), and worked as a songwriter and pit conductor on Broadway. There he met Max Steiner, who became a lifelong friend and collaborator. Arriving at Radio Pictures, Webb orchestrated the hit musical *Rio Rita* (1929), and Steiner joined him as head of the studio's music department in December 1929.

The Steiner and Webb team worked harmoniously at RKO. But Steiner loathed his required administrative responsibilities as head of the music department, and in 1936 he left RKO for the prestigious position of chief composer for David O. Selznick. This was followed by a long tenure as a composer at Warner Bros. Steiner's departure left Roy Webb as RKO's principal house composer, a position he fulfilled until after the studio was sold to General Tire in 1955. At RKO, music duties were essentially divided among Webb, who did most of the composing; the orchestrator Gilbert Grau, whose work was invariably uncredited; and Constantin Bakaleinikoff, who conducted and directed the orchestra while occasionally participating in the scoring of several films, including *The Fallen Sparrow* (1943).

Webb's main claim to cinematic fame remains his peerless score for Alfred Hitchcock's *Notorious* (1946), which Bakaleinikoff and Grau have both been given credit for orchestrating. The *Blood on the Moon* production records are mute on who orchestrated the score; they merely note that the overall budget for music on the film was $27,155. The music was brought in at $21,279.67, and over half of that expenditure was allocated to underscoring the opening and closing titles. According to composer and historian John W. Morgan, "The orchestration was by Gilbert Grau, RKO's general go-to in house orchestrator. I can confirm, as I looked at some of Webb's [compositions] at UCLA."[2] A case can certainly be made for Roy Webb as the quintessential film noir composer. His acute sensibility for music cues and underscoring, which complemented such films as *Murder My Sweet* (1944), *The Spiral Staircase* (1946), *The Locket* (1946), and *Out of the Past* (1947), remains unequaled. He also deserves much credit for the enduring success of the Val Lewton films. His Lewton scores conveyed the sense of suspenseful dread and dreaminess that the producer (along with the directors Robert Wise and Mark Robson) strove for despite the frugal RKO budgets. Webb composed the music for every Lewton-produced RKO horror-suspense film except *Isle of the Dead* (1945). A composer comfortable with any type of film, Webb also scored numerous Westerns for RKO over the years.

His score for *Blood on the Moon* heightens the mood and style of the picture. The underscoring of the film's opening titles conveys a sense of foreboding that seamlessly transitions to a pastoral cue as Jim Garry rides alone in the rain. Webb's score acts as a cinematic pathfinder, guiding the audience through all the meaningful scenes: sharp, staccato notes denoting the Garry-fired bullets humorously forcing Amy Lufton into the river, the bucolic cues accompanying long shots of Garry on horseback against the vistas of the Sedona valley, a brassy fanfare for the cattle stampede, and an ominous crescendo for the set piece fight sequence in the commissary saloon—all complementing the action on screen. Roy Webb's versatility allowed him to blend compositions accentuating the West's wide-open spaces with the anxiety-raising attributes of film noir.

As the picture was being prepared for release, screenwriter Harold Shumate surfaced, lodging a grievance with the Writers Guild, claiming he deserved screen credit along with Hayward and Glidden (under his pen name Luke Short). Even though most of his work had been expunged from the final script, Shumate—who had been around Hollywood a long time and knew how to play the game—was awarded a screen credit on *Blood on the Moon*.

Although Wise brought the picture in at $1,487,708.30—almost $200,000 over budget—there was no grousing by Schary, Rogell, or anyone in the front office. Wise's sure hand in managing the multiplicity of different units and filming locations, dealing with the unpredictable Sedona weather, and handling the actors, horses, cattle, wranglers, and stunt people was nearly faultless. But the RKO brass had many more things to be concerned about besides *Blood on the Moon*'s cost overrun, which was primarily attributable to a flawed budget that didn't consider the seasonal weather conditions in Arizona.

In 1947 the blacklist divided Hollywood into political satrapies of fear and loathing as the House Un-American Activities Committee (HUAC), under the dubious leadership of J. Parnell Thomas, began hearings into supposed communist infiltration of the motion picture industry. The so-called Hollywood Ten—a group of eight screenwriters, a producer, and a director who refused to testify—were cited for contempt of Congress. The studio heads, including Dore Schary, subsequently caved to political pressure from Washington with their "Waldorf Statement." This document linked continued employment in the movie industry to loyalty oaths amid sensationalist political polemics printed by Red-baiting ideologues, including *Hollywood Reporter* publisher Billy Wilkerson and gossip maven Hedda Hopper (who was fed confidential tidbits by her pal J. Edgar Hoover). They in turn were supported by people like director Sam Wood, the oafish actor Ward Bond, and other extreme right-wing members of the Motion Picture Alliance for the Preservation of American Ideals.

Schary was pressured to fire director Edward Dmytryk and producer Adrian Scott, who were both members of the Hollywood Ten and declined to answer HUAC's inquiries about their politics. Dmytryk and Scott had made *Crossfire*, RKO's biggest hit of the year, but it didn't matter. It was the beginning of a political purge of the entertainment industry that reached its somber apogee during the following decade.

The post–World War II box office slump was further exacerbated by the Supreme Court's *United States v. Paramount Pictures, Inc.* decision, announced May 3, 1948, which forced the "Big Five" movie studios to divest themselves of their movie theater chains because of Sherman Antitrust Act violations. Although it would take years for the studios to completely shed their theaters, this monumental shift, along with the emergence of television, would transform the motion picture industry.

More ominous for RKO was the acquisition of the studio by the aviation executive, pilot, and oilman Howard R. Hughes. Hughes, who bought 929,000 shares of RKO stock from Floyd Odlum on May 11, 1948, for $8.8 million, had been long been fascinated by Hollywood and the movies. He had produced *The Racket* (1928), the airborne spectacle *Hell's Angels* (1930), and *Scarface* (1932), a production that pitted him against Breen's PCA and various state censor boards that lined up against the controversial film. Hughes's production of *The Outlaw* (1943), characterized by his obsession with highlighting the contours of Jane Russell's breasts on screen, opened new vistas of discord between the eccentric mogul and the organization appointed by the studios to regulate movie content. Hughes's physical and mental health began a gradual decline after he crashed his experimental XF-11 aircraft into a Beverly Hills neighborhood on July 7, 1946. Given a fifty-fifty chance to live, Hughes survived but was horribly scarred and in constant pain; he subsequently became addicted to codeine. It didn't take him long to transform RKO from a movie studio into a plaything for his various obsessions.

Dore Schary's measured taste in movies, compared to Hughes's sensationalist yen, was equivalent to the cultural gap between a Shakespearean sonnet and a Sgt. Rock comic book. Schary attempted to talk Chairman Floyd Odlum out of selling RKO. Odlum wasn't a movie person; he was a sharp businessman who had foreseen the 1929 stock market crash, took his money out of the market, and built a $70 million business empire. He now foresaw what the future boded for the film industry and proceeded

Howard Hughes (seen here with Ava Gardner) regarded RKO Pictures as a plaything to indulge his fantasies (author's collection).

with the sale of the studio. After Hughes took control, Schary met with him. The new mogul's low-key manner and affirmation that nothing would change at RKO convinced Schary to stay put. The honeymoon lasted barely a month. In late June 1948 Hughes told Schary to cancel his passion production of *Battleground* because he thought a war picture wouldn't be popular and to fire Barbara Bel Geddes because her physical appearance didn't meet his expectations for a female movie star. Schary tendered his resignation the next day during a meeting at Cary Grant's empty beach house, where Hughes was staying. According to Schary, "The only sign of life was Hughes, who appeared from a side room in which I caught a glimpse of a woman hooking up her bra before the door closed."[3] Schary left on June 30, 1948, after purchasing the rights to *Battleground* from Hughes. After joining MGM in 1949 as production chief, Schary produced sixty-four pictures, including *Battleground*, which became Metro's top-grossing film in five years and was nominated for six Academy Awards, winning two.

RKO president Peter Rathvon exited two weeks after Schary. Hughes installed his own creatures on the lot, as he intended to make all major decisions at the studio, including reviewing and approving every script. RKO became the first Hollywood studio to fully concede to the government's consent decree by acquiescing to the dissolution of its movie theater chain. Hughes reckoned that he could sell more films to independent venues without the overhead of maintaining a network of theaters. The other moguls, including Darryl Zanuck and the brothers Warner, who were attempting to work out a compromise with the government to retain some of their theaters, felt betrayed.

Hughes fired more than half of the RKO workforce and canceled every picture in production except for three. Sid Rogell, who was named head of production by Hughes, had to figure out what to do about twenty-five actors with "play or pay" contract deals for forty movies that no longer existed. Although there was a backlog of films for release from the Schary regime, the studio's future appeared grim. Hughes next initiated secret investigations of his remaining employees to determine who were communists or were in any way disloyal to either America or him. His business operations were expanded to include a coterie of ex-cops, private detectives, and informers to spy on RKO employees, business rivals, and potential troublemakers while also keeping tabs on ingenues he had under personal contract, who were stashed like concubines at an assortment of Hollywood apartments and houses.

As RKO wrote off contracts worth millions of dollars and stacks of scripts were delivered to Hughes's office on Samuel Goldwyn's lot (the new RKO owner didn't deign to maintain an office at his own studio), the future of Robert Mitchum, the studio's brightest new star, was suddenly in serious jeopardy.

After completing *Blood on the Moon,* Mitchum discovered that his business manager, Paul Behrmann, had stolen all his savings less $58. Although Behrmann was a crook who eventually ended up in San Quentin, Mitchum's wife, Dorothy, had had her fill of Hollywood. Besides the vagaries of the movie business, she was fed up with her spouse's nocturnal carousing, accentuated by the continual availability of accommodating floozies and the offbeat assortment of characters Mitchum drank with and frequently brought home. On top of it all, they were now virtually broke. With Mitchum on a contractual layoff at RKO, he and Dorothy traveled back east and went to New York for a spell. When it was time to return to Hollywood to make another movie at RKO, Dorothy and the Mitchum children remained with her family in Delaware.

Robert Mitchum returned to an RKO with a new studio head and no movie for him. Despite Mitchum's burgeoning popularity, Hughes simply told him he would be in touch. Untethered from his family and without the discipline of work, the actor turned his already robust drinking and marijuana smoking into a full-time diversion. While looking for a new house with which he could lure his family back to Hollywood, Mitchum began hanging out with a starlet named Lila Leeds. She was a jaw-dropping beauty who turned heads but was better known for newspaper reports of assorted nightclub mayhem and being rushed to the hospital after an overdose of sleeping pills.

Around midnight on August 31, 1948, Mitchum, his pal Robin Ford, and another woman were at Leeds's rented Laurel Canyon bungalow ready to light up some joints when a pair of LAPD vice cops burst in

Attorney-fixer Jerry Giesler and Robert Mitchum at the Los Angeles Superior Court during the actor's initial appearance for his pot bust. After Mitchum pleaded guilty and served a brief time in jail, his popularity soared (author's collection).

and arrested all four of them for possession of marijuana. While being booked, Mitchum fessed up that he was a longtime pothead and maintained his characteristic sense of humor. Asked to provide his occupation, he replied, "Former actor."[4]

Not if Howard Hughes could help it. With RKO poised to release *Rachel and the Stranger* and *Blood on the Moon* later that year, he would vigorously protect his investment in Robert Mitchum by any means necessary. In his view, the actor wasn't anything really terrible, such as a communist. There are also grounds for the speculative belief that Howard Hughes secretly wanted to be Robert Mitchum, who was apparently living a roistering life free of the incessant Hughsian responsibilities of

"Like Palm Springs without the riffraff." Robert Mitchum serves his sentence at the Wayside Honor Farm in Castaic (author's collection).

running a business empire while fretting about germs and communists. The mogul envied Mitchum's ability to seemingly not give a damn while having any woman he wanted.

Hughes immediately dispatched a phalanx of lawyers to spring Mitchum from jail. He kept his star away from the press by stashing him in an RKO publicist's house. After canvassing his brain trust on whom he had to pay off, Hughes discovered he couldn't fix the case outright. Marijuana was viewed as a dangerous drug in 1948, and a possession bust was serious business. The newspapers were having a field day speculating that Mitchum was a sick addict who needed treatment. Although the LAPD was notoriously corrupt, it was seemingly resolute in breaking up the ring of drug pushers it claimed resided inside the film industry.

Hughes hired Jerry Giesler, the numero uno lawyer and fixer in town, to represent Mitchum. Carefully crafted press releases stressed the fact that the actor was innocent until proven guilty, and Dorothy and the kids were summoned to Hollywood for a photogenic family reunion. Giesler and Hughes understood that going to trial to fight the arrest could result in a string of revelatory headlines detailing Mitchum's licentious lifestyle. The LAPD had followed him for months before setting him up for the pot bust and was primed to enter the courtroom with skip loaders of dirt on the actor's personal life. Mitchum's popularity soared with his arrest, but who knew what might happen if his other peccadilloes became public?

On the advice of counsel, the actor offered no defense and was found guilty. Giesler hoped for probation for his client and got it, but it was a pyrrhic victory. The two years of probation for Mitchum and Lila Leeds included sixty days in the county jail. Giesler and Hughes arranged for his sentence to be served at the sheriff's Wayside Honor Farm in Castaic. By pure coincidence, Mitchum would do his time a stone's throw from the spot where months earlier he had been riding horses for Robert Wise in *Blood on the Moon*. Realizing his star was more popular than ever, Hughes visited Mitchum in stir and reassured him that RKO was with him one hundred percent. The mogul arranged a $50,000 loan so the actor could pay off his legal bills and buy a house for his family. Hughes also rushed production on *The Big Steal*, a Mitchum vehicle directed on location in Mexico by Don Siegel.

Amazingly, it all worked out. The legal calculations of Jerry Giesler combined with a subtle shift in cultural attitudes contributed to the public's giving Mitchum and his career a pass. After a world war that had killed millions, getting caught smoking a joint seemed trivial, even during an era when marijuana was generally believed to be a loathsome narcotic. The actor's calculated public expressions of regret and the PR campaign waged by Hughes certainly helped. But in the end, the reclamation of Mitchum's film career occurred primarily because of how appealing he was. People, especially women, simply dug him. He initiated the image of postwar cool on movie screens, and his pot bust notoriety consecrated his persona of roguish charm. Mitchum's turn as Jim Garry, the loose rider and fast gun with a personal moral compass that found true north with the wholesome Barbara Bel Geddes, reinforced his aura as the bad boy with a big heart.

Despite the continuing inanity of Howard Hughes's decision making at RKO, Mitchum never forgot how the oddball mogul stuck with him when he just as easily could have tossed him on the Hollywood scrap heap. Mitchum was now the studio's biggest star, and he reciprocated his boss's loyalty until his RKO contract ran out in August 1954. He referred to the increasingly reclusive studio mogul, however, as "the phantom."

9. | Aftermath

Robert Mitchum was released from jail on March 30, 1949, after serving forty-three days of incarceration. With typical aplomb, he described his time behind bars as resembling "Palm Springs without the riffraff."[1] The actor had reason to feel confident. *Rachel and the Stranger* and *Blood on the Moon* had been playing in movie theaters for five and four months, respectively. Both were solid box office performers for RKO during a year when theater attendance continued to decline. The reviews found *Blood on the Moon* praiseworthy. The reigning curmudgeon of movie criticism, Bosley Crowther of the *New York Times*, had this to say:

> *Blood on the Moon* still stands out from run-of-the-range action dramas. The reason is obvious enough. This picture has a sound, sensible story to tell and, besides, it is well acted. Robert Mitchum carries the burden of the film and his acting is superior all the way. . . . Lillie Hayward's screen play, taken from a novel by Luke Short, is solidly constructed and by not over-emphasizing Jim Garry's inherent honesty, she has permitted Mr. Mitchum to illuminate a character that is reasonable and most always interesting. The same can be said of the rancher's daughter, whom Miss Bel Geddes represents. Others who

> give worthy help include Walter Brennan, Mr. Preston, Phyllis Thaxter, Frank Faylen and Tom Tully. And a word should be said, too, for the direction by Robert Wise. A comparative newcomer to the directorial ranks, he has managed to keep the atmosphere of this leisurely paced film charged with impending violence.[2]

Variety also weighed in:

> *Blood on the Moon* is a terse, tightly-drawn western drama. There's none of the formula approach to its story telling. Picture captures the crisp style used by Luke Short in writing his western novels. . . . Picture's pace has a false sense of leisureliness that points up several tough moments of action. There is a deadly knock-down and drag-out fist fight between Mitchum and Preston; a long chase across snow-covered mountains and the climax gun battle between Preston's henchmen and Mitchum, Brennan and Bel Geddes that are loaded with suspense wallop.[3]

Robert Wise's next picture at RKO was *The Set-Up*, a boxing film he began shooting in October 1948. The preoccupied Hughes didn't interfere—probably because the notion of a boxing movie starring the virile Robert Ryan appealed to his testosterone-charged filmmaking perspective. The mogul's evolving modus operandi was not to intervene in a movie production until after the picture was completed. The finished film would then be held hostage by Hughes in his projection room for months as a blizzard of memos were sent to the producer, director, and head of the editing department recommending retakes, additional scenes, changing principal actors, and remaking endings, which Hughes invariably judged as inadequate. Director Richard Fleischer suffered having his 1950 film *The Narrow Margin* toyed with by Hughes for almost two years before it was released through a deal the director made with Hughes to direct a different finale for *His Kind of Woman* (1951). Before leaving RKO, Fleischer spent the better part of a year reshooting the ending of *His Kind of Woman* to Hughes's exacting specifications—which changed daily.

The Set-Up proved to be a masterpiece about the seamy side of boxing. It remains one of Robert Wise's best films and was one of his personal favorites. It was the first picture in which Wise used storyboards to sketch out all his shots in advance—a process he relied on for the rest of his career. His meticulous preproduction work—"I spent night after night doing research at the arenas around town"—and the stellar performances of Robert Ryan and Audrey Totter enabled the picture to win the Jury Award at Cannes.[4]

After finishing *The Set-Up*, Wise departed RKO for the greener pastures of 20th Century Fox. He put it bluntly: "I saw no future at RKO after Howard Hughes bought the studio and needed to get out." Darryl F. Zanuck and his Fox team had been impressed by Wise's A film debut and quickly inked him to a multi-picture, nonexclusive contract. Wise remembered *Blood on the Moon* as "invaluable to me because it got me signed at 20th Century Fox." He directed a number of impressive pictures at Fox, including *The Day the Earth Stood Still* (1951), before forming a production company with his former RKO colleagues Mark Robson and Theron Warth for *The Captive City* (1952), shot entirely on location in Reno, Nevada.

During the next two decades, Wise navigated the rocks and shoals of a changing Hollywood with great skill. With few exceptions, he exercised astute judgment on the properties he chose to direct and produce.

Forty-three years after *Blood on the Moon*, Robert Wise and Robert Mitchum are reunited in Hollywood (author's collection).

The grim captivation of *I Want To Live!* (1958) and the groundbreaking *Odds against Tomorrow* (1959) would be contrasted with the huge mainstream successes of *West Side Story* (1961) and *The Sound of Music* (1965). Wise won Academy Awards for the latter two films as Best Director and Best Picture, and won the Irving Thalberg Memorial Award in 1966. He became one of America's most influential and honored film directors and rarely made the same type of picture twice. As he put it, "I sought different colors in my [cinematic] palette." He made only one other Western, *Tribute to a Bad Man,* in 1956, starring the redoubtable James Cagney.

His numerous honors include the American Film Institute (AFI) Life Achievement Award in 1998. Wise also served as president of the Directors Guild of America and the Academy of Motion Picture Arts and Sciences and as chairman of AFI. He directed his last feature in 1989 and a final television movie in 2000, at the age of eighty-six. A tireless contributor and nurturer of young filmmakers, he provided film seminars to students at more than twenty universities until his death in 2005 at the age of ninety-one. Wise's mentorship of young filmmakers was vitally important, as there were no longer any intimate movie studios like RKO at which young people could work their way up from the loading dock to the director's chair.

Howard Hughes continued to run RKO into the ground. In March 1949, stockholders approved a split of the theater arm of the company from the movie production unit. Ironically, the theater unit was the only profitable RKO component at that point. Under Hughes, film production slowed to a crawl. The 1949 production slate press release ushered in his practice of announcing films that would never be made. In 1950 Sid Rogell was fired after telling Hughes to perform a difficult anatomical act during the last of a series of interminable late-night phone calls from the insomniac mogul. RKO produced fifteen films that year. Hughes hired the prestigious production team of Jerry Wald and Norman Krasna, who were stymied by Hughes's irrational micromanaging and departed the studio after four films. Samuel Bischoff arrived and left as head of production as the studio suffered a mass exodus of talent; agencies were recommending their clients not sign with RKO. Hughes's studio continued its downward trajectory toward bankruptcy, by one reckoning losing $100,000 per week.

After waging a legal battle against screenwriter Paul Jarrico and the Screen Writers Guild after he removed Jarrico's screen credit for *The Las Vegas Story* (1952) over alleged communist ties, Hughes sold the studio in 1952 to a group of investors with links to organized crime. In a plot twist worthy of a film noir, the cabal eventually had to return Hughes's RKO stock and forfeited its $1.25 million down payment as the studio posted a loss of more than $5 million. Hughes bought all of RKO's outstanding stock in 1954 for $23,489,478 and then turned around and sold the studio for a final time to General Teleradio, a subsidiary of the General Tire and Rubber Corporation. The new company mined RKO's film archive for its chain of television stations while sparking a spasm of resurgence in film production that lasted less than a year.

In 1957 the RKO production facilities in Hollywood and Culver City were sold to Desilu, a television company established by former RKO contract actress Lucille Ball and her husband, Desi Arnaz. Before he submitted his final bid of $6,150,000 to General Tire, Arnaz telephoned none other than his former landlord Howard Hughes for advice. The now nearly stone-deaf ex-mogul yelled at Arnaz over the phone, "Grab it, Cuban! Buy it, or I shall! At that price, you can tear them down and make them both into giant parking lots. You've gotta make money!"[5] Hughes moved on to his next obsession: Las Vegas. After buying up a good portion of the town's resort hotels, he descended into a reclusive existence in a series of shuttered hotel suites, injecting himself with codeine and watching iterative screenings of *Ice Station Zebra* (1968). The bedridden billionaire died in 1977 after years of mental and physical decline accentuated by malnutrition and drug addiction. RKO's Hollywood lot was eventually absorbed by the adjacent Paramount Pictures. The former Pathé lot in Culver City changed hands numerous times and is currently being leased by Amazon.

As for Fred Glidden, his determination to write novels and wait for Hollywood to come to him paid off. After serving in the Office of Strategic Services during World War II—he was rejected by the army because of his poor eyesight—Glidden became well-off from sales of his writing. He liked to attend high-profile boxing matches and maintained a string of racehorses even as sales began to diminish in the late 1950s, when magazines like *Collier's* went out of business. His spec screenplays

Fred Glidden's former house is a designated city landmark in Aspen, Colorado (courtesy of Aspen Historical Society; all rights reserved).

were rejected, a thorium mine venture failed, and his work was frequently plagiarized. During the 1960s, his contract with Bantam Books ended, his son James drowned in a tragic accident, his longtime agent and his brother both passed away in the same year, and his eyesight began to fail. Despite these personal and professional setbacks, Glidden remained active, helping found the Western Writers of America and becoming deeply involved in the community affairs of Aspen, Colorado, including serving a term on the city council.

After writing six more novels in the 1970s, Frederick Dilly Glidden, better known as Luke Short, succumbed to throat cancer on August 18, 1975. His legacy of Western novels, with more than 26 million copies sold, earned him the deserved moniker "the dean of Western writers."

The American Western reached its cultural zenith during the 1950s. The genre traveled both forks in the evolutionary road as the B serials of heroic, shoot-'em-up oaters migrated into television with episodic shows like *The Lone Ranger* and *Hopalong Cassidy*. Western features began their new route to the big screen as Anthony Mann folded some noir elements from his *T-Men* (1947), *Raw Deal* (1948), and *Border Incident* (1949) into a pair of noir-stained Western melodramas, *The Furies* (1950) and *Devil's Doorway* (1950). Mann followed with a series of Westerns at Universal starring James Stewart, whose hard-bitten protagonists of *Winchester '73* (1950), *Bend of the River* (1952), *The Naked Spur* (1953), and *The Man from Laramie* (1955) made Jim Garry appear more like an easygoing cowpoke. Director Budd Boetticher and writer Burt Kennedy reinvented Randolph Scott's screen identity as a revenge-seeking former sheriff in *Seven Men from Now* (1956) and a Jim Garry–like cowhand who blunders into a cabal of murderous outlaws in *The Tall T* (1957) as part of a series of popular films starring Scott. Even the work of John Ford shed much of its sentimentality with *The Searchers* (1956). Most of the Mann Westerns were especially interesting for the dichotomy between the characters and stories, which were definitely cast in noir in the tradition of Mann's cinematic oeuvre at Eagle-Lion, and for the visual look of the films, all of which after *Winchester '73* were in color. These pictures proved that you could remove the noir sensibility from the city and transplant it into the wide-open spaces of the West, but shooting a picture in color, rather than in black and white, and at night, as Wise did in *Blood on the Moon*, creates a movie that is demonstrably more Western than film noir.

The variety and perspective offered by televised Westerns expanded as they literally took over the national ratings by the end of the decade. Of the top-ten-rated television programs of 1958–1959, seven—*Gunsmoke, Wagon Train, Have Gun—Will Travel, The Rifleman, Maverick, Tales of Wells Fargo,* and *The Life and Legend of Wyatt Earp*—were Westerns.

Film noir traveled a different path to arrive at a similar destination. The bow wave of the postwar noir phenomenon began to crest in the early 1950s as a number of movies transposed the characterizations of the noir city into the country and back again. Lonely big-city copper Jim Wilson (Robert Ryan) is brutalized by his job patrolling rain-slicked city streets in *On Dangerous Ground* (1951). "Garbage, that's all we handle!" fulminates a furious Wilson as he is prevented by his partner from beating hell

Ida Lupino and Robert Ryan in *On Dangerous Ground* (1951). By the early 1950s, several films blended urban noir and the West in a round-trip transition (courtesy of Film Noir Foundation).

out of yet another suspect. When he is exiled to the northern country, a wilderness covered in snow, to investigate a murder, he ends up pursuing a pathetic kid—a psychopathic murderer of a young girl—accompanied by the deceased child's father (Ward Bond), a revenge-obsessed dullard. As Wilson falls in love with the killer's blind sister (Ida Lupino), he discovers that though this latest crime might be more senseless, the country and the city are essentially identical. Hard-bitten urban reporter Chuck Tatum (Kirk Douglas) finds himself in a different situation in *Ace in the Hole* (1951). On the skids professionally, Tatum corruptly manipulates a man's being accidentally trapped in an underground cliff dwelling in New Mexico (filmed in Gallup, the location of numerous Westerns, including *Pursued*) into a front-page story he believes will propel him from the backwater of the *Albuquerque Sun Bulletin* back to the big time of New York City newspapering, where he can nosh on kosher pickles and hobnob with Yogi Berra at Toots Shor's. Tatum discovers that his capacity for hypocritical deceit has a moral breaking point as his orchestration of events inevitably causes his own destruction. The subterranean attributes of the West that Chuck Tatum believed would be the locale of his salvation turn out to be a nothing more than a mirage.

In the late 1940s, the influence of World War II remained pervasive as several films merged the country and the city with the creation of postwar suburbia. *Act of Violence* (1948) relates the story of a war veteran turned successful housing contractor with a hidden past (Van Heflin) who is married to the gorgeous Janet Leigh. He lives and works in the burgeoning suburbs and goes fishing in the nearby country until his past catches up with him in the personage of an ominous, limping Robert Ryan, who pursues him from his home into the bowels of the city. Heflin's horrific wartime betrayal of his fellow soldiers in a German prisoner of war camp is eventually exposed as he goes berserk on the trash-blown streets of downtown Los Angeles. Heflin is forced into an alliance with a coterie of disreputable nocturnal creatures, including an aging prostitute (Mary Astor), a con man (Taylor Holmes), and a killer (Berry Kroeger) in a fruitless attempt to save himself from Ryan's justifiable payback.

The visual aspect of noir in black and white with low-key lighting began to give way to authentic noir narratives filmed in color and/or wide-screen CinemaScope, including *Black Widow* (1954), *I Died a Thousand Times* (1955), *Violent Saturday* (1955), *House of Bamboo* (1955), *Slightly Scarlet* (1956), *A Kiss before Dying* (1956), *House of Numbers* (1957), *Man in the Shadow* (1957), and *Party Girl* (1958). These films were thematically dark, but the studios were desperate in deploying an array of Technicolor, CinemaScope, VistaVision, and Cinerama offerings—anything to pry patrons away from their television sets and back into movie theaters. Westerns and films noir were affected by the brief fad of 3D movies in 1953–1954. Westerns were at a popular high during that period, with or without the 3D gimmickry of *Hondo*, *Gun Fury*, *The Stranger Wore a Gun*, *The Moonlighter*, and *The Charge at Feather River* (all 1953), as well as *Southwest Passage* and *Taza, Son of Cochise* (both 1954). Film noir was sparsely represented in 3D by *I, the Jury*, *Man in the Dark*, and *The Glass Web*, all released in 1953. Of this trio of mostly unmemorable films, only *I, the Jury* boasted the shaded black-and-white visuals of ace noir cinematographer John Alton.

The postwar film noir phenomenon began to peter out by 1958 with *Touch of Evil*, *The Lineup*, and *Murder by Contract*. Noir began to seep into television. A striking instance of the transferal of noir from the movies to TV and back again was *He Walked by Night* (1948). The Eagle-Lion film noir policier inspired Jack Webb's *Dragnet* on radio and then television, which in turn resulted in Webb's theatrical feature production of *Dragnet* (1954) from Warner Bros. Since noir is not a genre, its transference to television was more subliminal. Televised crime shows, courtroom dramas, and police procedurals, including *China Smith*, *M Squad*, *Johnny Staccato*, *77 Sunset Strip*, *Peter Gunn*, and *Perry Mason* owed their existential style to many of the literary creators of films noir who ended up writing for television, including A. I. "Buzz" Bezzerides, Roy Huggins, and Jonathan Latimer, accompanied by actors who made their bones in noir, such as Dan Duryea, Raymond Burr, and Lee Marvin. The assembly-line production of movies by the major studios, particularly second features, gradually ended. Independent films filled some of the void, particularly with low-budget horror and science fiction movies shown at drive-ins for an increasingly teenaged audience. The second features and B movies of film noir and Western serials were eventually replaced by episodic television series.

Blood on the Moon was the celluloid bridge that facilitated the transference of the Western movie genre and the film noir movement to emerge as a commingled forerunner of the stylized Westerns that would dominate American cinema and television during the next decade. The film's pictorial and narrative artistry represented RKO Pictures at its pinnacle of creativity, just before the studio's precipitous decline and eventual ruin under Howard Hughes.

It was the movie that put Robert Wise in the forefront of emerging film directors at the beginning of the end of the Hollywood studio system. It is arguable that without *Blood on the Moon,* there would have been no Wise-helmed masterpieces such as *The Day the Earth Stood Still, I Want To Live!, Odds against Tomorrow, West Side Story,* or *The Sand Pebbles.* Talent alone was and is never enough in Hollywood. Wise could have ended up like his friend and colleague Theron Warth, whose career essentially ended in 1953, or—worst case—Val Lewton. *Blood on the Moon* established Robert Wise as a bankable, A list director, and we are all much the better for it.

Blood on the Moon anointed Robert Mitchum as perhaps the most appealing male movie star of the post–World War II era. The picture wouldn't be what it is without Mitchum's performance. His screen image of handsome, bemused indifference never camouflaged his serious professionalism as a unique actor—professionalism that shone through in several of the bad and yet retrospectively entertaining films (he called them "gorilla pictures") that Howard Hughes subsequently put him in. Jim Garry remains one of Robert Mitchum's most authentic and enjoyable characterizations.

Finally, the film remains the finest screen adaptation of the work of Frederick Dilley Glidden (a.k.a. Luke Short), who was one of the most influential and popular Western writers of the twentieth century. Despite the lengthy evolution from book to film, *Blood on the Moon* established the viability of Glidden's work both in print and on screen. It remains a consequential film that ranks with the best American Westerns of the twentieth century.

ACKNOWLEDGMENTS

I am extremely grateful to these dedicated librarians and archivists for making pertinent research materials available for this book during an extremely challenging period for all libraries and archives:

Molly Haigh at Special Collections, Charles E. Young Research Library, UCLA

Warren Sherk, Kristine Krueger, and Louise Hilton at the Margaret Herrick Library, Academy of Motion Picture Arts and Sciences

Lauren Goss at Special Collections, University of Oregon libraries. (A particular merci beaucoup to Ms. Goss, who scanned and sent the requested Glidden correspondence free of charge!)

Sandra Garcia-Myers at the USC Cinema Arts Library

I would also like to thank selected friends and colleagues for their specific contributions and support:

My pal Brian Light and Armand at LP Transfers 4 U for their invaluable transfer of Robert Wise's *Blood on the Moon* laser disc commentary to DVD. Brian also provided the image of the Italian

Blood on the Moon poster from his impressive collection of vintage movie posters.

The late Bertrand Tavernier, who loved *Blood on the Moon* and sent me his essay on the picture shortly before his untimely passing. This book is dedicated to Bertrand, whose joy of film was contagious.

An astute chronicler of Hollywood's history and my good friend Philippe Garnier, who translated Bertrand's essay while adding his own insightful and acerbic comments.

The indefatigable Tom Weaver for his research assistance.

My dear friend Scott Eyman, who read the manuscript and offered typically excellent suggestions.

The one and only Leonard Maltin and David Williams at *American Cinematographer* for the image of Nick Musaraca.

Thomas J. Doherty at Brandeis University for the image of Joseph I. Breen.

Anna Scott at the Aspen Historical Society for the images of Frederick Dilley Glidden.

My colleague Robert Nott, who initially told me about the University of New Mexico Press and the Reel West series.

Peg Goldstein, whose copyediting acumen is second to none.

Steven Hull and Andrew Nelson at the University of New Mexico Press.

NOTES

INTRODUCTION

Unless otherwise noted, all quotations attributed to Robert Wise were sourced from his commentary track on the *Blood on the Moon* laser disc, Turner Entertainment, 1990.

1. "Draft introduction to *Blood on the Moon*," Bertrand Tavernier to author, email, December 27, 2020. Translation by Philippe Garnier.
2. Garfield, *Western Films*, dedication.
3. Christopher Wicking and Barry Pattison, "Interviews with Anthony Mann," *Screen* 10, nos. 4–5 (July 1, 1969): 10.
4. Production Code of 1930, "Reasons Underlying the General Principles," paragraph 2.a.
5. Joseph I. Breen to Jack L. Warner, Production Code Administration letter, January 19, 1938, Warner Archive, University of Southern California, Los Angeles.
6. Thomas Doherty, *Hollywood's Censor: Joseph I. Breen and the Production Code Administration* (New York: Columbia University Press, 2007), 83.
7. Lee Horsley, *The Noir Thriller* (London: Palgrave Macmillan, 2016), 91.
8. Horsley.
9. Jon Tuska, *Dark Cinema: American Film Noir in Cultural Perspective* (Westport, CT: Greenwood Press, 1984), xvi.
10. Robert Porfirio, "No Way Out: Existential Motifs in the *Film Noir*," *Sight and Sound* 45, no. 4 (1976): 212–17.
11. Lee Server to author, circa 2007.
12. James V. D'Arc, *When Hollywood Came to Utah* (Layton, UT: Gibbs Smith, 2019), 78.

13. Richard Armstrong, Tom Charity, Lloyd Hughes, and Jessica Winter, *The Rough Guide to Film: An A–Z of Directors and Their Movies* (New York: Rough Guides, 2007), 136.

CHAPTER 1

1. "Luke Short—Western Story Writer," *Pulp Flakes*, August 17, 2012, PulpFlakes.Blogspot.com/2012/08/luke-short-western-story-writer.html#more.

2. *Missouri Alumnus*, September 1931.

3. *Missouri Alumnus*, September 1931.

4. "Luke Short (1908–1975): The Dean of Western Writers," *West of the River*, http://westofriver.blogspot.com/2013/11/luke-short-1908–1975-dean-of-western.html, accessed February 21, 2021.

5. "Brian Garfield Interview," *Pulp Serenade*, September 16, 2011, http://www.pulp-serenade.com/2011/09/brian-garfield-interview.html.

6. "Draft introduction to *Blood on the Moon*," Bertrand Tavernier to author, email, December 27, 2020. Translation by Philippe Garnier.

CHAPTER 2

1. Marguerite Harper to Frederick Glidden, May 23 and May 28, 1941, Frederick D. Glidden Papers, University of Oregon.

2. Harold Shumate, *Gunfighter* script, September 30, 1941, RKO Collection, Charles E. Young Research Library, UCLA.

3. H. M. Swanson to Marguerite Harper, December 31, 1941, Frederick D. Glidden Papers, University of Oregon.

4. Frederick Glidden to H. M. Swanson, n.d., Frederick D. Glidden Papers, University of Oregon.

CHAPTER 3

1. Lasky, *RKO*.

CHAPTER 4

1. David Wise would become RKO's studio manager in charge of infra-

structure and fixed assets that were not films. His name is appended to *Blood on the Moon* production memoranda relating to the coordination and staging of trailers, portable dressing rooms, trucks, cameras, sound booms, and similar impedimenta that supported his brother's direction of the picture at the RKO ranch facilities in Encino and Castaic, California, and Sedona, Arizona.

2. Rode, *Charles McGraw*, 59.

3. Leemann, *Robert Wise on His Films*, 21.

4. Siegel, *Val Lewton*, 40.

5. The late Stanley Rubin, who produced *The Narrow Margin* (1952) under Sid Rogell's supervision, told me the executive producer reminded him of a "nightclub bouncer." Mark Fleischer, son of director Richard Fleischer, who learned the hand-to-hand combat realities of movie studio politics under Rogell, remembered that as a kid he would spit out the window of his father's car when passing RKO Studios, chanting, "Sid Rogell, son of a bitch." Mark Fleisher in conversation with the author.

6. Siegel, 56.

7. Charles Koerner is best remembered as the man who fired Orson Welles while coining the motto "showmanship instead of genius"—a sarcastic barb aimed at Welles's ballyhooed reputation. Conversely, he hired Val Lewton, returned RKO to profitability, and was the most successful studio boss in RKO's tumultuous history. No less a cinematic artist than Jean Renoir mourned Koerner's passing as the death of "an extraordinary man . . . who knew the business and the exploitation of cinema, but at the same time conceded one must experiment." Jean Renoir, interview by Jacques Rivette and François Truffaut, *Sight and Sound*, July–September 1954.

8. Siegel, *Val Lewton*, 71, 66.

9. Leemann, *Robert Wise on His Films*, 71.

10. Val Lewton to Ben Piazza, RKO interoffice communication, September 11, 1944, Robert Wise Collection, Special Collections, University of Southern California, Los Angeles.

11. Siegel, *Val Lewton*, 82.

12. Leemann, *Robert Wise on His Films*, 74.

13. Bosley Crowther, "The Screen," *New York Times*, May 1, 1947.

14. Leemann, *Robert Wise on His Films*, 78.

CHAPTER 5

1. Stephen S. Jackson, PCA, to Harold Melniker, December 18, 1947, MPAA/PCA Collection, Margaret Herrick Library, Academy of Motion Picture Arts and Sciences, Beverly Hills, California.

2. Stephen S. Jackson, PCA, to Harold Melniker, February 16, 1948, MPAA/PCA Collection, Margaret Herrick Library, Academy of Motion Picture Arts and Sciences, Beverly Hills, California.

3. Leemann, *Robert Wise on His Films*, 83–84.

CHAPTER 6

1. Server, *Robert Mitchum*, 56.

2. Server, 96–97.

3. Roger Ebert, "Out of the Past," RogerEbert.com, July 18, 2004, www.rogerebert.com /reviews/great-movie-out-of-the-past-1947.

4. Lillie Hayward, *Blood on the Moon*, final script, February 12, 1948, RKO Collection, Charles E. Young Research Library, UCLA.

5. Barbara Bel Geddes official website, http://www.barbarabelgeddes.com.

6. David Richards, "Robert Preston, with a Capital P," *Washington Post*, July 22, 1984.

7. Richard Erdman in conversation with the author, circa 2011.

8. Rollyson, *A Real American Character*, 23.

9. Lillie Hayward, *Blood on the Moon*, final script, February 12, 1948, RKO Collection, Charles E. Young Research Library, UCLA.

10. Server, *Robert Mitchum*, 148.

11. Eric Schaefer, "On Musaraca," *Film Reference*, www.filmreference.com/Writers-and-Production-Artists-Me-Ni/Musuraca-Nicholas.html.

CHAPTER 7

1. RKO Radio Pictures production report, *Blood on the Moon*, February 14, 1948.

2. RKO Radio Pictures production report, *Blood on the Moon*, February 17, 1948.

3. RKO Radio Pictures production report, *Blood on the Moon*, February 23, 1948.

4. Lawrence Bassoff, *Crime Scenes: Movie Poster Art of the Film Noir* (Beverly Hills: Lawrence Bassoff Collection, 1997), 11.

5. Jane Greer to author, May 26, 2001, at an Egyptian Theatre book signing.

6. McNeill, *Arizona's Little Hollywood*, 376.

7. *Blood on the Moon* shooting script, page 21, February 12, 1948, Robert Wise Collection, University of Southern California, Los Angeles.

8. *Blood on the Moon* shooting script, page 129, February 12, 1948, Robert Wise Collection, University of Southern California, Los Angeles.

9. RKO Radio Pictures production reports, *Blood on the Moon*, March 25–27, 1948.

10. RKO Radio Pictures production report, *Blood on the Moon*, March 12, 1948.

11. RKO Radio Pictures production reports, *Blood on the Moon*, April 15–20, 1948.

CHAPTER 8

1. *Blood on the Moon* final script, February 12, 1948, 86, 91.

2. Steven C. Smith, email to author, November 19, 2021.

3. Longworth, *Seduction*, 287.

4. Server, *Robert Mitchum*, 167.

CHAPTER 9

1. Server, *Robert Mitchum*, 193.

2. Bosley Crowther, "Mitchum Carries New Cowboy Thriller," *New York Times*, November 12, 1948.

3. "Blood on the Moon," *Variety*, December 31, 1948 (misdated 1947), https://variety.com/1947/film/reviews/blood-on-the-moon-1200415883/.

4. Leemann, *Robert Wise on His Films*, 87.

5. Lasky, *RKO*, 2.

BIBLIOGRAPHY

Bartlett, Donald L., and James B. Steele. *Howard Hughes: His Life and Madness.* New York: W. W. Norton, 2004. (Originally published in 1979 as *Empire: The Life, Legend, and Madness of Howard Hughes.*)

Borde, Raymond, and Etienne Chaumeton. *A Panorama of American Film Noir, 1941–1953.* Translated by Paul Hammond. San Francisco: City Lights Books, 2002.

Carringer, Robert L. *The Making of Citizen Kane.* Berkeley: University of California Press, 1985.

Dickos, Andrew. *Street with No Name: A History of the Classic American Film Noir.* Lexington: University Press of Kentucky, 2002.

Fenin, George N., and William K. Everson. *The Western, from Silents to Cinerama.* New York: Orion, 1962.

Gardner, Gerald. *The Censorship Papers: Movie Censorship Letters from the Hays Office, 1934–1968.* New York: Dodd, Mead, 1987.

Garfield, Brian. *Western Films: A Complete Guide.* New York: Da Capo Press, 1982.

Jewell, Richard B. *RKO Radio Pictures: A Titan Is Born.* Berkeley: University of California Press, 2012.

———. *Slow Fade to Black: The Decline of RKO Radio Pictures.* Oakland: University of California Press, 2016.

Jewell, Richard B., and Vernon Harbin. *The RKO Story.* New York: Arlington House, 1982.

Jordan, Joe. *Robert Wise: The Motion Pictures.* Rev. ed. Orlando, FL: BearManor Media, 2020.

Keenan, Richard C. *The Films of Robert Wise*. Lanham, MD: Scarecrow Press, 2007.

Lasky, Betty. *RKO: The Biggest Little Major of Them All*. Englewood Cliffs, NJ: Prentice-Hall, 1984.

Leemann, Sergio. *Robert Wise on His Films*. Los Angeles: Silman James Press, 1995.

Longworth, Karina. *Seduction: Sex, Lies, and Stardom in Howard Hughes's Hollywood*. New York: Custom House, 2018.

McNeill, Joe. *Arizona's Little Hollywood: Sedona and Northern Arizona's Forgotten Film History, 1923–1973*. Sedona: Northedge & Sons, 2010.

Meuel, David. *The Noir Western: Darkness on the Range, 1943–1962*. Jefferson, NC: McFarland, 2015.

Rode, Alan K. *Charles McGraw: Biography of a Film Noir Tough Guy*. Jefferson, NC: McFarland, 2008.

Rollins, Peter C., and John E. O'Connor, eds. *Hollywood's West: The American Frontier in Film, Television, and History*. Lexington: University Press of Kentucky, 2005.

Rollyson, Carl. *A Real American Character: The Life of Walter Brennan*. Jackson: University Press of Mississippi, 2015.

Selby, Spencer. *Dark City: The Film Noir*. Jefferson, NC: McFarland, 1984.

Silver, Alain, and James Ursini, eds. *Film Noir Reader*. New York: Limelight, 1996.

Silver, Alain, and Elizabeth Ward, eds. *Film Noir: An Encyclopedia Reference to Film Noir*. 3rd ed. Woodstock, NY: Overlook Press, 1992.

Server, Lee. *Robert Mitchum: Baby, I Don't Care*. New York: St. Martin's Press, 2001.

Short, Luke. *Blood on the Moon*. 1941. Reprint, New York: Bantam Books, 1948.

Siegel, Joel E. *Val Lewton: The Reality of Terror*. New York: Viking Press, 1973.

Simmon, Scott. *The Invention of the Western Film: A Cultural History of the Genre's First Half-Century*. New York: Cambridge University Press, 2003.

Smith, Imogen Sara. *In Lonely Places: Film Noir beyond the City*. Jefferson, NC: McFarland, 2011.

Tuska, Jon. *The Filming of the West*. Garden City, NY: Doubleday, 1976.